LILLYANNE

MEMOIRS OF
THE PEOPLE'S MEDIUM

PAULA BAIRSTOW

Text Carole Richardson, on behalf of Story Terrace

Design Grade Design and Adeline Media, London

Copyright © Paula Bairstow

First print March 2019

www.StoryTerrace.com

CONTENTS

1

CHOSEN

Sitting among the gravestones in Whitkirk Churchyard, it came as no surprise to me when a blonde-haired, rosy-cheeked little girl appeared by my side.

"Hello," she said.

Smiling straight at her, I replied, "Hello!"

"You can see me, can't you?" she added.

It was more of a comment than a question, but I nodded anyway and told her I could. I didn't bother to mention that I could also see right through her ghostly child's body.

Then, without another word, she disappeared again, much faster than her shiny red shoes could have carried her. Long before we had had the chance to become friends. Completely unfazed, I turned my attention back to the bread and butter 'picnic' I'd brought with me from home.

Even though I can't have been much older than six or seven, I was so used to seeing people nobody else could that I didn't bat an eyelid. If it hadn't been her, it might have been the stern-looking elderly lady in the long black dress who'd popped out to see me. Or maybe the gentleman with the walking stick who was always whistling.

It never crossed my mind to be scared of the strangers I'd become so used to seeing on a daily basis. It had been happening for as long as I could remember. The first time was in my mum and dad's bedroom, but they came from all over and I would chat to them, quite naturally, about everyday things. Some were human spirits; some were from another planet altogether. It seemed to me even then that I had much more to be afraid of with living humans…

Growing up in the 1960s and 70s in Woodland Road, Halton, a nice area on the east side of Leeds, I spent the first 10 years of my life living in relative working-class luxury compared to most of my friends at home and at school.

I use the word 'friends' loosely because it seems that almost from the moment I was born, on 17th September 1964 in St James's hospital in Leeds, I was different. Singled out. Chosen. In more ways than one. And it didn't exactly help me to fit in, either at home or at school, which is how I came to spend any free moment I could sitting alone in the nearest graveyard.

At home – a Catholic household – I was the second child and only living daughter of Joseph and Pauline Joyce. My elder brother, Dale, was 18 months older than me, but it was Anthony, who was 13 months younger, who I was closest to. After him came Christopher, who I was also close to and who was to become crucially important to me years later.

My fourth and youngest brother, Stephen, was six or seven years younger than me and we never really had much in common.

Between Anthony and Stephen there'd briefly been a sister, Angela. Tragically, at 14 months old she had somehow slipped down her coat and asphyxiated.

As young as I was, I can remember the commotion in our house when the police were called. They complained because the light bulb wasn't working in my mum and dad's bedroom, where Angela's cot was, and they had to use flashlights. It is probably one of my earliest memories.

My own bedroom was across the landing. Barely a box room, it could fit a single bed and a chest of drawers but not a wardrobe as well. The walls were covered with pink flowered wallpaper and to jazz it up further, I used to tie ribbon bows, woollen pom-poms and flowers made of scrunched-up coloured tracing paper all over the place. I can't remember who taught me how to make the pom-poms. It could well have been *Blue Peter!*

What I really loved about that room was the big window looking out on to the long back garden. I could spend hours gazing out there, up at the sky (I've always been attracted to the sky and the stars and planets), or at the big old oak tree at the bottom of the garden, where I could see my special friends, the ones I could – and still can – always rely on. My Star People.

What I hated about that room was the privacy it gave me. And my dad…

2

"OUR SECRET"

As the date of my first Holy Communion approached, my dad arrived home one day with a big pink box and a beaming smile on his face.

"This is for you," he announced as he proudly handed it over to me.

Excitedly, I tore off the lid to pull out the most gorgeous white dress. It was like a miniature wedding dress complete with a slim fitting bodice and a full length puffed skirt. It came with a veil held in place by artificial flowers and was every little girl's dream. Mine included.

There and then, I stripped down to my knickers and vest and tried it on. It was an absolutely perfect fit.

"Give us a twirl, Paula," Dad ordered, and I happily spun round and round and round, feeling like a little princess.

Only my mum's frosty reaction spoiled the moment.

"It's too much, Joe," she complained, referring to the cost.

Although she was snobbish enough for our family to stand out in the neighbourhood, she didn't like the idea of me attracting too much attention when I took my first Holy Communion with my class from St Theresa's Catholic Primary School in Cross Gates.

Hmmm. I wonder why? After all, it was all right for everybody to know we were the first family in the street to have a Bush colour telly and a telephone. They could hardly avoid knowing if they'd walked past our three-bed council semi during the daytime, when the front room curtains were always pulled back wide enough for all to see our carefully displayed status symbols.

Well, tough! I was going to have my big day – and I did. Even now, I'd still say I was the best dressed girl there! I felt a million dollars.

I'd been christened Paula Michelle at St Patrick's Catholic Church at nearby Harehills, and it followed that I would go to St Theresa's at Cross Gates when I was of school age.

Although we very rarely went to church on a Sunday as a family, I loved the Catholic religion; despite my work as a psychic medium today, I still have a lot of time for it.

St Theresa's was a very strict Catholic school, but I loved it there as well. Even on my very first day I didn't cry, unlike some of the other girls. One, Julie, was so frightened and sobbed so much that she made herself sick.

I was fine, though I never liked the nuns, who taught us and who ruled the place with a rod of iron. Despite them, I still felt like I belonged there, in my neat navy uniform. Never more so than when we were sitting down in class rows in assembly, or in nearby St Theresa's church, to which we made regular trips. There was always some holy day or other to celebrate.

Most of my classmates hated those times, but I loved them. No wonder they thought I was different to them. I had friends, but I can't say I really fitted in. I rarely got invited to birthday parties.

I adored singing and loved all the hymns in assembly, especially the carols at Christmas time. Even now, when you might hear Slade or The Pogues being played in neighbours' houses during the festive season, it's always classical music you'll hear coming from ours.

In church, I just loved the sense and feel of the place. I loved the smell of the incense; I loved saying Our Fathers and Hail Marys. I even liked just sitting quietly and praying. It's true to say that I felt 100 percent more comfortable there than at home.

More than once or twice, it crossed my mind to tell one of the priests – Father Tagney or Father Whiteside – about Dad. I thought about the times he would come into my bedroom carrying a toilet roll and put his hand down my knickers while masturbating, and I wanted to ask them, "Is that wrong?"

It could happen morning, noon or night. Sometimes I'd be asleep and he'd wake me up. A drinker, he always smelled of alcohol – gin, I think – and cigarettes. I can't honestly pinpoint when it started, but as far as I am aware it went on all my life, until I reached 15 and a half.

I do know that I hated it. I absolutely hated it.

"Remember, Paula," he'd always remind me. "This is our secret. You know you love being here with your brothers. Let's just keep it our secret."

So I did. For far too long.

3

PLAYING A BLINDER

Pointing down to the bottom of the garden at my strange-looking gang of friends gathered round the oak tree, I'd ask my mum, "Can you see them?"

"Oh yeah," she'd reply every time. "Go outside and play with them."

And, as if it was the most natural thing in the world, I'd run off to chat to my Star People, not thinking that there was anything to be embarrassed about or feel frightened of. These were my real friends, much more so than the kids I went to school with.

Ever since I looked up into the sky one day when I was four or five years old, I've been promised that they will protect me. They've always been true to their word.

It all happened out of the blue. One minute I was watching the clouds float past from my mum and dad's bedroom window; the next a big face was glowing directly down at me from the clouds.

I was too young to know who Elvis Presley was but, with

hindsight, the face looked just like his, complete with thick black hair and bright piercing eyes. I was used to seeing people appear suddenly and vanish just as quickly – it had been happening for as long as I could remember. There were always groups of young children, grandmas and grandads who didn't belong to our family – or, often, to any family on this earth – in my mum and dad's bedroom. I'd chat away to them about what I'd done at school or how I loved going to church. But they always came in droves. Here, before my eyes, was the very first single spirit I'd ever seen.

And suddenly he started talking to me.

"We are always going to look after you," he promised.

Back then, of course, I didn't know what I needed protecting from or why I needed looking after. Apart from the confusing problem with my dad, the first 10 years of my life were very happy. I can't pretend otherwise.

Curious, I asked him, "Where are you from?"

"We are called Star People, and we are from up there," was the answer, delivered by a huge grandfatherly figure who stepped forward out of nowhere to answer me and point upwards to what we'd call Heaven. And as fast as the faces in the sky appeared, they disappeared.

After that, these very tall, very slim people with startling bright green or blue eyes that glowed like stars became an everyday part of my life. Compared to the spirits of dead people that I usually saw, I suppose they looked quite biblical.

Remember the old Ready Brek adverts on telly? The Star

People have a glow all round them just like the kids had after eating their cereal. Only the Star People's aura is turquoise blue. Their faces are rounder than ours and their jaws are heavy, but they have slimmer noses and smaller mouths than us. Their clothes are just the same as yours or mine though. The men wear suits, apart from one who wears robes and has lots of brown wavy hair. Except for that first occasion, they always turn up in groups. Sometimes three or four but sometimes 20 or 30, like a big orchestra. My safe gang. From another dimension altogether. I've always felt completely at home with them. I still do.

As the manager of a local betting shop, my dad had a lot of respect in the community and we were the bee's knees in Woodland Road. He was a wheeler dealer who loved rummaging round charity shops, and that meant that he was an excellent provider. He always seemed to know where he could get his hands on things.

So when the kids on the street were having beef burgers for their dinner if they were lucky, we could be having fillet steak. We wanted for nothing at all. Especially me.

In many ways his extreme generosity towards me created a problem with my three brothers. I soon became aware of their frostiness because of it.

"How come Paula gets all this and we get nowt?" they'd ask when he'd come home with something or other for me.

As the only girl, I was never going to get hand-me-down clothes or shoes like them. My shoes came from Clarks and my outfits were always brand new. But did I really need the suede coat he bought me or the red and white trouser suit with the fancy decorative chain, which made me the smartest little girl around in the early 1970s?

"Oh you know Paula!" (Or Polly, as I was sometimes called.) "She's got her daddy wrapped round her little finger," my mum would say to anybody who would listen when my lavish outfits were remarked upon.

I grew up used to hearing her tuts and disapproving comments about me when it came to my dad 'spoiling' me. Just as I was used to hearing her voice from the next bedroom shouting out, "Hurry up Joe!" whenever he was doing whatever he was doing to me. Back then I didn't know exactly what he was doing. But she knew. She absolutely knew.

As for me, although I'd never been told it was wrong, deep down I knew something was not right. But I also knew that my dad loved me, and that he kept me clothed and fed.

It just felt a bit odd that he was showing me his willy. Odd enough to mention it to my Star People, who I knew were safe and nice. I never told my mum or my brothers, though. That was too much of a risk.

"They'll tell me if it's wrong,' I told myself over and over, trusting the Star People to give me the truthful answer.

"We can't interfere with it, but we will always support you. Remember the face you saw in the sky," was their reply.

It sounds mad, I know. But with God as my judge, I am telling the truth. Whenever I needed support, I knew exactly where to turn.

"We are here for you, Paula," they'd repeat, time after time. And they always are, even today. Even when I can't see them, I can feel them, sense them and even smell them around me: a mix of frankincense and rose oil.

I can't say for 100 percent certain that my dad abused me from the day I was born. As far as I know, it went on all my life until the middle of my 15th year.

Amidst all my confusion, my dad was still my dad. I watched telly with him: *Black Beauty* or *Dial M for Murder, Appointment with Fear* and *Tales of the Unexpected* (which I was probably far too young for). I loved him and trusted him. He was my hero and he absolutely adored me. Nothing he could do for me was too much. It was all about Paula with him – the boys didn't get a look in. It was the other way around with Mum.

Even so, I dreaded his visits – sometimes during the day, but mainly at night. I was his plaything at least four times a week. If I wasn't already awake, the feel of his hands going into my pyjama bottoms and knickers would wake me up.

"Remember, I am not forcing you to do this," he'd tell me from when I was about six or seven.

But I detested it, and the underlying threat was always there: if I told anybody about this, I would be taken away from my family.

"You know you love being here with your brothers, you like to see your brothers. Let's just keep it our secret."

"I have never ever forced you to do anything, have I, Paula?"

Looking back, I was conditioned to say no. In my own

head, there was also the added worry that if I was taken away, I might not be able to go to church any more. So the silence continued, and to the neighbours we must have looked like a nice ordinary family; a lovely little Catholic family.

At that stage of my life, every day seemed to start with a big pan of porridge on the stove in the kitchen. After that, I'd walk the mile and a half to school along a busy main road with two of my brothers.

At school, I liked drawing and reading about places from olden times. I wanted to know what Calvary looked like and about the history of Bethlehem. I loved reading and I was at the top of my class at St Theresa's for the subjects I liked – English, Drama, Art. In fact I didn't hate any of the lessons.

I always walked home alone and would find Mum, who worked as an auxiliary nurse on a geriatric ward, already in the kitchen cooking tea. There was always something in the oven. She was a good cook and always making and baking things. Often I'd stand and watch her. I still find myself making the same meals from scratch that she did: bangers and mash, corned beef hash, shepherd's pie. Sundays were usually roast beef and Yorkshire puddings. Even now, if I'm frying bacon, I always sling in some chopped tomatoes, just like she did, for extra flavour. I've never tried baking bread like her, though. People would bring cigarettes round in exchange for some of her bread.

In many ways, they were happy days. I can't honestly say I

was neglected in any way, shape or form – even though, when I look back now, I do feel robbed of my innocence and my childhood. All lost. But if you take the issue with my dad out of the equation – wow. Wouldn't it have been a great upbringing?

My mum kept the house immaculate and there was always good food on the table. On Fridays when Dad got paid, she would take me to the Queens supermarket with her and if I was lucky I got to choose a bar of chocolate. At other times, she'd take the lads with her.

"I don't want to stop at home, Mum," I'd plead.

"No, you stay there. Go and sit on your dad's knee."

Oh, she knew what was going on all right…

Often my aunties and uncles would come round on Friday and Saturday nights, and there'd be music and drinks. 'The Book of Love' or 'Pretty Woman' would be playing downstairs while I hovered around the landing, seeking security in the company of my brothers.

Christmas was always brilliant. We'd have stockings with an orange, fruit, nuts and chocolate inside and my real presents would be under the bed. One year it was a Tiny Tears doll and a beautiful navy blue Silver Cross dolls' pram. I felt like the bee's knees pushing that around the neighbourhood, when I wasn't playing hopscotch or whip and top.

My dad's parents were of Irish descent. They were real characters who had no airs and graces. I never liked my Grandad Peter, who died of lung cancer when I was seven or eight years old and who I have no nice memories of. He was a drinker and a gambler who used to smack my hands whenever I sucked my thumb. I adored my Grandma Ellen though, who always had a big pie or something in the oven or Club biscuits for us whenever we went to visit her. What luxury!

Something always drew me more to her than to my mum's mum, Grandma Mary, who was very prim and proper. Yet apparently, it was Grandma Mary's mum, Great-Grandma Smith, who is thought to have worked in a shed on Blackpool seafront reading crystal balls. I can't say for certain whether it's true, but in her mid-20s she's said to have discovered her psychic edge. Perhaps it's not so surprising then that, despite being a staunch Catholic, my own mother was into crystals and had them dotted around the house. She was certainly very intuitive, there's no doubt about that. She always sensed when somebody was poorly or something was wrong.

Acting on it was a different matter, though – at least in my case.

Living opposite us was an elderly couple, Mr and Mrs Sweeney; their son-in-law was the late actor Colin Welland, who won an Oscar for his *Chariots of Fire* screenplay and a Bafta for his role as the teacher in *Kes*. Whenever Colin or their grandchildren visited, I'd go over to play. They were an extremely kind family.

Whenever I could, though, I'd make an excuse to escape from home and walk the five minutes to Whitkirk Cemetery, where I felt at peace among the graves, the gorgeous flowers and the spirits who regularly popped up to see me. I still feel most at peace in a graveyard, even today.

Every summer in those early years we went on holiday for a week in a caravan at Primrose Valley, in the North Yorkshire seaside town of Filey. I spent hours making sandcastles and playing with my brothers on the beach. The sea scared me, though. It still does. I find it a bit overpowering.

Strangely, I was never actually scared of my dad. It was like he was two different people: in public, this same man who came into my bedroom at night was a very respectable figure who worked hard six days a week, was always suited and booted in well-pressed trousers and a shirt, and would do anything to help anybody in the community.

My mum was a very tiny, lovely looking woman with backcombed blonde hair. She was always smartly dressed and wore sharp pointy shoes. But she had a coldness about her. There was always a sinister feeling around her that I didn't like.

Years later, a detective would say that she had 'played a blinder'. Looking back, I can see that he was absolutely right. It's obvious to me now why she went along with my friendship with the Star People, never questioning it for a minute – encouraging it, even. It suited her because if I ever opened up to anyone outside the family and my dad's secret behaviour came out, she could always tell everybody that I was the doolally one who spoke to dead people. 'The Twisted Sister', as I later became known to my brothers. It made perfect sense.

While turning a blind eye to the moral rights and wrongs

of the situation, she was busy working out her own carefully calculated plan for if and when it all hit the fan. Even when I went to her with a terrifying problem that no little girl still at junior school should ever have to worry her head about, she quickly had her own damage limitation plan in place. My own mother. Shame on her.

4

AM I PREGNANT?

Knowing that my mum was washing up in the kitchen on her own, I picked my moment to blurt out what was bothering me.

"Mum, I've got something to tell you…" I began nervously.

"What's up now?" she demanded, no doubt expecting me to start another conversation about my Star People.

"I think I might be pregnant," I announced, aged 10.

She took one look at me, and suddenly she couldn't control herself. It was as if somebody had just told her a massive joke. I can still hear the roar of her hysterical laughter.

"Stop being so bloody silly. Your Star People can't get you pregnant," she managed to say to me as she dried her hands on the tea towel, all while I stood there feeling awkward and stupid.

"For you to get pregnant, you have to have full sexual intercourse with a man," she added by way of an explanation.

Looking back, she seemed very sure that full intercourse had not taken place between me and my dad. So of course the idea of me carrying my own father's – her husband's – child was all a big joke, no real threat at all because she knew he hadn't actually penetrated me and that I hadn't yet started my period.

My sex education had come from Jennifer, Beverley and Mandy, girls a couple of years older than me who lived nearby, and had taken place when we were all outside playing on our estate's little triangular-shaped green. They'd frightened the life out of me by talking about willies and how they could get you pregnant if they went anywhere near you. It had alerted me to the terrifying fact that when my dad was rubbing up against me (as he'd progressed to doing by now), the white stuff that ran down his leg was somehow connected to babies. Nothing had been mentioned of any need for menstruation on my part, and I'd panicked. My mind had gone into overdrive. I can vividly remember standing there on the green and freezing inside, thinking, *He never told me that! What am I going to do now? Who do I tell? If I say 'owt, I will be put in a home. And if I am pregnant, my mum is going to ask, "Who's the dad?" What am I going to tell her?* Round and round went the thoughts in my head. I couldn't stop them. I had absolutely nobody human to turn to – only my Star People. And they couldn't physically interfere with what was going on, as they kept reminding me.

If I am honest, my mum's reaction, callous as it was, reassured me. At 10 years old, I was vaguely aware of the birds and the bees thanks to the playtime gossip, but until my mum actually explained it to me, I hadn't been 100 percent sure of the facts.

Sex education wasn't a subject that was even on the curriculum at St Theresa's, where I was probably the smallest girl in my class and one of the last to physically mature. I'd always been a picky eater and, as such, only a slip of a girl. At one point, I had been put under the care of a hospital weight specialist. I can remember my mum shovelling fruit malt loaf into my mouth before appointments. At around five foot 10, and stockily built, my dad would have made at least two of me. On many occasions I screamed and tried to fight him off, but I didn't have a prayer.

Embarrassed, but relieved to be told that I couldn't be pregnant, I headed into the living room to double check with my dad that what my mum had told me was true.

"Dad, all this stuff with us, does it mean I could be having a baby?"

"Absolutely not!" came his categorical reply, and I let the subject drop for the time being. But a couple of days later I brought it up again after he'd 'visited' me in my single bed, where I'd been scrunched up into a ball, dreading him coming in.

"I've already told you once. Don't be silly," he snapped.

But I can also remember how sad and pitiful his eyes were when he looked at me. It was as if he knew what he was doing was wrong, but he just couldn't help himself.

Not long afterwards, maybe a couple of months or so, I was lying in the bath when my mum came in. Complaining to her that my 'minnie' was red and sore, she took a look between my legs. Not for the first time.

"Does it itch?" she asked. When I nodded, her suggestion was to scratch it with a toothbrush, as she did when she had a similar problem. Urgh.

Even at that age I knew it wasn't a good idea, and eventually she agreed to take me to the doctor with my embarrassing little problem, which she pushed off as an infection. But I knew what was causing it and I've no doubt she did as well.

The doctor agreed that my genital area looked sore, and as well as advising me to wipe carefully after using the loo, he gave me a big white tube of cream. I can't remember the name of it, but the writing was blue and it was to provide vital damning evidence years later.

Never one to miss an opportunity, my cunning mother also decided to tell the doctor about my conversations with my Star People.

"She's hearing voices, Doctor," she informed him – the first time she had done so, though it wouldn't prove to be the last. Clever. Now it was on my medical records that I was the strange one who spoke to the dead, and it could be used to discredit me at a later date should I speak out about my abuse. It was as if she was saying, "Joe, I've got your back covered here." Cold, calculated and methodical.

"Who do you talk to, Paula?" the doctor asked, and I told him.

"I think there's something not right about her, Doctor," Mum said.

It was a ruse that she would make use of several times over

the next few years. I can remember one doctor – another male GP – reassuring her, "She's perfectly normal. She's just got imaginary friends."

Well, he might have been a very intelligent and highly educated man, but he got the second bit wrong. My Star People were never imaginary. They were just always there for me, as they still are. They would pop up from behind, usually, and open my spiritual door. I loved them and relied on them to keep me alive and sane. Their job was always to make sure that I didn't have a mental breakdown, which could so easily have happened if it hadn't been for them supporting me, being always on my side.

No matter how sore I was or how many tubes of cream I went through, nothing stopped my father from abusing me four or five times a week. I tried my best to get into my brothers' bedroom to sleep with them, but my mum and dad would never allow it.

I was so wrapped up in all my own worries that the possibility of something being wrong with my parents' relationship with each other never even entered my mind. I never saw them shouting or screaming at each other, as you might expect from a couple on the brink of splitting up.

And even though it seemed odd that a couple of my dad's pals sometimes came round while he was at the betting shop, I never put two and two together. Even though I was told to stay downstairs while they went upstairs with her. I think she was in debt to one of them for some coal.

So it came as a complete surprise to me when one day, around March time in my final year at St Theresa's, my dad came in from work and started packing a big grey suitcase full of his stuff. I can remember the time of year because the pink blossom tree in the garden was in full bloom when the taxi arrived for him.

"Polly, I am going to live with your Nanna Ellen. Hopefully you'll be able to come and live with me at some point," he announced.

Then the front door closed behind him and he was off. The funny thing is – and it sounds crazy – I was heartbroken as well as relieved when my dad was leaving. I was frightened to death of my mum and felt she'd pick on me now, but I was glad that I might be able to start sleeping with my brothers. I loved the bones of my brothers.

Almost immediately, whole crowds of my Star People appeared at my left-hand side. They always turn up there. It's as if they're permanently there, on guard, even when I can't see them.

"It will be OK. You are going to be OK, Paula. Don't be worrying," they reassured me. "We are not of Earth. We can't interfere with this, but we will always keep you of sound mind. We will always look after your mind."

Things went downhill dramatically after my dad left. Within minutes of his departure, all home cooking was phased out as my mum hit the drink. She was soon knocking back milk stout in the house at all hours, and we were left to eat Golden Wonder crisp sandwiches and an apple for tea. I can't remember her getting us up for school. Our clothes got scruffier and my brothers would scavenge for biscuits in the bins behind the Queens supermarket. My most vivid memory of that time, though, is of booze and multiple men coming into the house at all hours – including a 14 year-old who was sleeping with her against the law.

We stayed in Woodland Road for a while after the split and it was horrendous. There was nothing to eat and my mum was a thorough bastard to me. No doubt about it.

"You won't be getting new clothes anymore," she seemed to enjoy telling me.

Just because he'd gone to live at our nanna's didn't mean we'd seen the last of our dad, though. Often a taxi would roll up late at night and he'd arrive from the Squinting Cat pub in Swarcliffe, often drunk. How I hated that familiar tap-tap, tap-tap-tap knock of his at the front door, because I knew what to expect next.

"Paula, your dad's here,' my own mother would shout from her bedroom, indicating for me to open the door to him. Often my brother Chris had climbed into bed with me so that he could protect me, but it didn't make any difference. They'd both just drag him out, with my mother saying, "Your dad is getting in with her." They must have had an exceptionally close bond, those two.

Social services must have been brought in at one point, as I have a vague recollection of Dale and Anthony being put under care orders. I remember my dad going mad about it, but he needn't have worried. Somehow 'our secret' went under their radar.

Eventually we were evicted, presumably because some of the neighbours reported her to the council for all the parties she was holding. The news was dropped on us like a bombshell. Dale, Anthony and I were all in the living room when my mum declared, "We are moving to be amongst people that are more like us."

What does that mean? I can remember thinking. *Are there loads more kids whose dads do this to them?*

Despite everything, I was sad to be leaving my bedroom with the fantastic view and the pink blossom tree. But most of all, I was worried about my Star People. Would they come too?

Thankfully, I needn't have worried. They soon appeared, as they always did at a time of crisis, to reassure me. "We are coming with you. We will be with you for rest of your life."

A big removal van arrived, and we were piled into the back of it with the furniture we had left to move to a new house on another Leeds estate. I think the red velvet three-piece suite had been flogged by then.

What a shock we got when we pulled up outside number 37 Kendal Road, Halton Moor. It was awful. Freezing cold, bare floorboards and an outside toilet. A dark, empty place.

"Don't worry, it won't be forever," promised my Star People. "We will always be here. We will always support you. We will always make you strong."

If that house was a wake-up call, there was another just around the corner: my first day at Osmondthorpe Secondary School. I'd always assumed I'd go to St Bridget's with everybody else from my class at St Theresa's, which I'd been sorry to leave.

Anthony and I turned up together, and I couldn't believe the swearing I was hearing or the people who were openly spitting on the floor. Silly things I'd never experienced at school before. And everybody looked so scruffy.

Before long, my dad was a regular visitor once again. Often he'd leave a pair of tights or the change from his pocket or a Mars Bar for me on the mantelpiece. Sometimes it would be all three. As always with his gifts, there was a price to be paid, and I can remember crying the day I first heard the word *prostitute* and realised what it meant.

"Does that make me a prostitute?" I can remember asking my dad.

"No," he assured me.

His abusive behaviour became more advanced at Kendal Road, and by the time I was 12 he was lying on top of me and simulating sex while making me promise that as soon as I was 16, I would give him my virginity. I didn't know what the word virginity even meant. When I asked, he told me, "One day I will put this fully inside you and I will be the first man to do it."

Quick as a flash, my Star People were there to reassure me. "That will never happen, Paula."

Living in a house that never had any food in the cupboard meant that I looked forward to a big Sunday roast at my Nanna Ellen's – my dad's mum – every week. Even the hour-long walk to her house from Halton Moor didn't deter Anthony and me from getting to her table.

Afterwards, my dad would go drinking at the Squinting Cat pub in Swarcliffe. When he got back he'd go for a lie down and shout for me to join him. Automatically I'd head up the stairs, despite my nanna's advice: "Don't follow your dad."

I can't say for sure that she knew what was going on, but it's possible because she was always telling him, "Joe, leave Paula alone." She'd also say to me, "Why do you always run upstairs when your dad, calls Paula? Stop following him."

I was embarrassed. How was I supposed to stand up for myself and say no in the face of the threats of what could happen to me? Once, when I was staying overnight, there was even an argument between the two of them. Nanna Ellen insisted, "She's sleeping with me," and tucked me up tight in her own double bed with her.

What I didn't know then was that my father had been abused by his own father. In spite of – or maybe because of – his own past, the abuse carried on into another generation and, by 13, I was expected to perform oral sex on him.

"It's all legal and above board. And when you're a bit older, Paula, I can take you to Africa and marry you and no other man can touch you. We're allowed to get married in Africa," he told me.

"It's not going to happen, it's not going to happen," repeated my Star People. I had to believe them.

Meanwhile, life at Osmondthorpe Secondary was a fight for survival. I wasn't thick by any means, but I didn't thrive there. I still loved English, Drama and Art, and I can still remember a pencil drawing I did of David Bowie from the Aladdin Sane album cover going up on the classroom wall. I loved David Bowie. I also loved Biology, seeing how the human body worked and where all the organs were placed. It was an interest that seemed to run in my family. My mum was a nurse and was also a medium. She was very spiritual, and she was a massive influence in my own spiritual life. She really, really was. She loved anything witchy. Despite her having been christened Catholic like my father, I never saw crucifixes in the house; instead, she had ornamental witches and crystals. Even my children can remember that. I've still got some crystal ornaments that she gave to me. She loved Indian music as well. Could she hear people from the other side? Yes, she could.

Her father, my Granddad William, was a paramedic; my cousin is a pharmacist and my brother Dale is a fitness instructor. That natural interest stood me in good stead for my specialist psychic work today, using the spirits to pick up on illnesses in people and heal where I can. Even at school, people would come to me with a cut knee or a banged head. I'd place my hand over it, saying, "It'll be OK in a minute."

And within no time they'd be marvelling, "It's OK now, Paula! How do you do that?"

At 13, I changed schools and went to Parklands High in Seacroft. It was nicer there and the teachers were nicer. Without a coat to my name I was freezing cold in winter, and one of the dinner ladies, Vera, took pity on me and brought me one that her granddaughter had grown out of. What a lovely woman.

Parklands was also just a 10 to 15 minute walk from my dad's betting shop. Sometimes my mum wouldn't give me the bus fare home or any food, so if I wanted to get home or eat, I had to call there. And so the abuse continued, as did the threats.

At 14 he physically tried to rape me, but stopped when, bleeding and hurting, I begged and begged him to. Things were moving on, and it was somewhere around this time that I snapped and told my mum what was going on.

I can remember thinking, *She's got to know this,* and deciding to wait until all my brothers were home before confronting her.

"Mum, I've got something to tell you. I want you to know about this," I began nervously, before going on to explain that my dad had been coming into my bed and abusing me all my life. I'll never forget her reaction.

"*What?*" she screamed. "You f***** lying little bastard!" Dragging me downstairs and knocking me around the house, she yelled to my brothers, "'Have you heard what this sicko is saying about your dad? She's absolutely f***** twisted."

They all laughed, and after that I was called Twisted Sister.

As ever, my Star People were there to reassure me that I'd get through this, and it was around this time that I made what I always call my 'deal' with them. They wanted to use me as a channel for good, but they gave me the ultimate decision about whether I wanted to work with them. Of course I agreed, knowing that it would become my career path.

Although I absolutely believe that I was 'chosen', I don't believe that I am special. Different, but not special. If anything, when I was younger I felt alienated because of my psychic abilities, and I didn't like it. But at 15 and a half, I met and fell in love with my first boyfriend, who was two years older and a friend of my brother Dale. He was my saviour.

I knew things couldn't continue the way they were with my dad. I felt angrier than ever, and I confronted him.

"Pack it in now. You've done enough. You are not controlling me anymore. I've got a boyfriend and it ends now."

The look of fear, shock and horror on his face said it all. Nevertheless, he continued to threaten me.

"Nobody in your lifetime will ever believe you," he warned. However, obviously worried about what might come out one day, he left me alone after that.

Freed from his abuse, I began earning a couple of bob here and there doing readings for people. Locally, I'd become known as the quiet, crazy girl who could speak to dead people.

"Your dad is sitting at the side of you, and he wants you to know that the cancer has gone," I told one friend of a friend.

And with another – a 15-year-old girl who'd just had a

miscarriage – I could reassure her that the baby was being taken care of by an auntie in spirit. I've always loved reassuring people, just as my Star People have always reassured me that things will work out – even though, at times, it's been difficult to see how.

They show me events from the other side, and I pass the information on. I've always known when illness or a funeral is around the corner for someone. That medical intuition has never left me, and sometimes it's been a hard burden to bear.

My new boyfriend was a lovely guy who I went out with until he dumped me at 17. I was devastated. He was the lead singer in a band, and I'd been the talk of the school when we first got together. Everybody wanted to be on his arm, but it was me he chose.

My last year at school was hit and miss attendance-wise, and I left at 16 with no qualifications and no money. When my dad offered me a job as an accounts clerk in his betting office, I had no choice but to take it: if I didn't, I knew that my mum would kick me out onto the street. I think I probably worked for him and another bloke for three to six months without anything happening. No meant no.

Ever the Catholic girl, I thought that my boyfriend and I were going to get married. Although he was the first boy I had an intimate relationship with, I can't say I enjoyed it. It meant nothing to me and didn't impress me.

"Is that it, then?" I remember asking him after the first time.

Despite this, being close to another male, who I could talk to and trust, was important to me – but very gently, he let me down. At the beginning he would see me three or four times a week, but gradually it became less and less until I was seeing him for maybe an hour a week, at which point he told me it was over.

I didn't get back with him, but around this time I did bump into the men who would be my future first and second husbands – David Jones and Martin Flay – though of course I didn't realise it then.

As I was walking up the stairs of The Adelphi, a pub in the city's student area of Headingley, one Friday night, the two of them were on their way down and David said, "I'm glad I've seen you. Do you fancy a night out next Friday?"

Although he was seven years older than me – 24 and newly out of the Army – I agreed. Looking back, it shouldn't really have happened, but I was scared of my dad and I suppose, if I'm completely honest, I wanted another man in my life to protect me. So we hung around together for a few weeks, an intimate relationship began and I got pregnant. Just like that.

Dave was an absolute gentleman, but I knew in my heart of hearts that I didn't love him. I'd just made the biggest mistake of my life. However, without wishing to be judgmental to anyone who's had an abortion, I didn't personally believe in it and would never have gone through with one myself.

"When you are given a baby, it's a gift from God," I remembered hearing from the priests at church and school. It has stuck with me to this day.

So, that was how I came to be sitting back in my GP surgery with my mum. In those days you did your test there and then and the receptionist gave you the results. Pressing his intercom button, the doctor asked the receptionist. "Can I have the pregnancy test result for Paula Joyce?"

"It's positive, Doctor," she announced to the three of us over the loudspeaker. I looked at my mum and she looked at me. Still only 17 but a whole seven years after my first scare, it seemed that this time, I really was pregnant.

St Theresa's Catholic Primary School 1974 (I am in the front row, second from the left)

5

OUT OF THE FRYING PAN...

When I confronted the father-to-be with my news, it was evident from the word go that he was absolutely elated. Unlike the mother-to-be...

Hotfooting it from the doctor's surgery to the butcher's shop where David worked, I came straight out with it. "I've been to the doctor today. I'm pregnant."

Shocked but over the moon, he burst into tears on the spot. Now, as relieved as I was that he was the father of my child, and as aware as I was that my situation could have been so much worse, any tears I might shed were not going to be for joy.

I am not going to lie: I was devastated to be saddled, at 17, with a baby and marriage. There was never any question that David wouldn't do 'the right thing' and, not wanting my baby to be illegitimate, which was so much more of a stigma back then, I wanted a ring on my finger and matching surnames on the birth certificate. Respectability. I craved it.

So, eight months pregnant, wearing a long, loose-fitting purple and gold hippie dress and carrying a bunch of red roses from my mum, I became Mrs Paula Jones at Leeds Registry Office in July 1982. Afterwards our families celebrated the marriage with a reception at a local pub paid for by David's stepfather Brian, who was also a butcher I think. The meat was good anyway!

I think David thought he'd got me for life. He absolutely adored me. But while I did feel something for him, I wouldn't say it was true love. Unlike the feeling I got when I took one look at our beautiful baby girl four weeks later…

Charmaine was born a month before my 18th birthday at St James's Hospital (popularly known as Jimmy's due to widespread TV coverage) on 5th August 1982, after a 24-hour labour with no pain relief. It was the most natural thing in the world.

I took one look at her, she looked at me, and I was ecstatic. I was so protective of her it was unreal. During the five or six days I was in hospital, I clung to her cot. My mum wanted to take her off me, adopt her, so that I would be free to have a life and she could have a baby for her and the much younger husband she'd since acquired. She had no chance! I wouldn't even let the nurses take my baby girl off to the nursery at night to give me a rest, as they liked to do with new mothers. It wasn't hard to see why. Fair haired with very pale skin and dinky blue eyes, she was gorgeous. All 6lb 9oz of her.

Dave absolutely adored Charmaine, who he called 'Little Charlie', just as he adored me. But from the word go, the marriage never really got off the ground. If I am completely honest, even on our wedding night I knew that I'd done the wrong thing. Sadly for him, it wasn't long before I left him, taking Charmaine with me. He was a good man: kind, caring and genuine, who'd never recovered from the death of his father. I felt sorry for him, but I'd clearly made a mistake, so I had to tell him honestly: "I can't live with you like this anymore." I've never regretted the decision, but I'm not proud of the pain it caused him. It would have been cruel and wrong for me to stay with him, but I know it broke his heart and that later he took his own life, which is another story. (After the birth of her first son, Charmaine decided she wanted to be reunited with her dad and I managed to locate him through his stepfather Brian. I spoke to him first, telling him that Charmaine wanted to see him, and he was absolutely over the moon. He told me he'd kept an eye on us over the years. She wouldn't speak to him on the phone, saying she'd rather see him face-to-face, so I arranged a meeting between them at a Kentucky Fried Chicken restaurant in Armley or Wortley. One or the other. However, she changed her mind and decided she didn't want to see him after all. And that absolutely devastated him.)

The plain truth is that something had always intrigued me about his more attractive friend with the cheeky grin, Martin Flay. He was something of a risk taker, and he had something about him that I liked. Unfortunately, David had been the first one to ask me out that night when I'd bumped into them both in the Adelphi.

So it was to Martin I turned when I left David, and his flat soon became our next home. My Star People, though still all around me, remained silent. They know that their place is not to judge.

Time would prove this to be another big mistake, and it was very much a classic case of *out of the frying pan and into the fire*. I'd escaped my dad and Martin was the better of the two evils, but let's just say it was a relationship beleaguered with problems. It was certainly not a happy one. Martin Flay was a violent bully who, years down the line, was jailed for brutally attacking his two sisters Paula and Deborah after they refused to give him money. I spent the next 10 years with him living on tenterhooks.

"Hang on, hang on. One day, Paula, you will have your say," my Star People repeatedly reminded me. "Don't worry, we will always keep you of sound mind."

On the bright side, my relationship with Martin, who I married after my divorce from David was finalised, did produce six of my eight children. I love them all to this day, but it's true to say that I am prouder of some than others. Sadly, two of my treasured sons are no longer on this Earth plane, but they have not deserted me altogether. Far from it.

I fell pregnant with my first baby boy soon after getting together with Martin, and he was absolutely over the moon at the prospect of becoming a dad. When, aged 19, I gave birth to Martin – named after his father – back at Jimmy's hospital on 6th May 1984, he was besotted with his son.

Credit where it's due, Martin loved all his children and, just as my own father had been, he was a good provider. In the early days he worked long hours in a slaughterhouse as the babies came in thick and fast. Before Martin's first birthday, Katy had arrived six weeks prematurely after a very traumatic pregnancy. And before *her* first birthday, John had arrived, bless his soul. Joanne, Ashley and Demi followed. Always on hand to help out with babysitting and general care was my own mum. She helped a lot, and to her credit, she was more than just a good grandma: she was an excellent one. I cannot deny her that. Although what her motive was, I still can't say for sure. Guilt? Possibly, but I like to think that she actually had feelings for me, her only daughter. Years down the line though, the police had their own theory, which had more to do with manipulation in case the truth about my childhood abuse ever came out.

As my family continued to grow, so did my reputation for giving readings, and soon I was giving two or three a week. It got to the stage where complete strangers, recommended by friends and acquaintances I'd impressed, would come up to me and ask me to read for them.

To set the record straight, I must explain first and foremost that I am a spiritualist medium, not just a psychic or a fortune teller. At one point I briefly used rune stones and tarot cards that I bought from a shop under the Dark Arches near the railway station in Leeds. But I don't need tools. Unlike a psychic – and I really believe that we are all born psychic but that it is up to us to expand and develop it – a spiritualist is somebody with a direct link to the other side. My Star People are my link.

Secondly, I have never ever called my special ability a gift. It's not. It is very intense, hard work and at a professional level, it's a very bitchy business. More than one rival has tried to ruin me. They know who they are...

Even with clients, you know you will be constantly tested. People always want more, and it can be emotionally gut-wrenching. It can be heart-breaking. Some of the horrors I've seen in spirit...

On the other hand, it is overwhelmingly beautiful when you can tell somebody whose mother has passed from cancer that she's OK. I can remember one very nervous young woman coming to my Leeds flat. If I had to guess, I'd say she was probably around 22 or 23, but other than that I knew nothing at all about her and that's the way I like it. Unlike some mediums, I never give the initials of spirits to the people I'm reading for. Spirits don't work in initials.

I couldn't actually see the young woman's mother in spirit, but I could sense her energy and I could hear her speaking. She was so glad that she'd managed to connect to me and that she was able to pass on messages to her daughter, who was elated when I managed to calm her down and tell her about her mother's passing six months earlier due to cancer. I described the funeral and one or two other big events that were very personal to their lives.

But what convinced her that I really was in touch with her mum was the fact that I kept getting an overwhelming smell of perfume as I passed on the messages. I recognised it as that one I sometimes used: Anais Anais. Apparently it was her mum's favourite perfume and she never left the house without it on. At the end of our session, she left tearful but happy and relaxed. On the way out, she gave me a massive cuddle and couldn't thank me enough. I've never forgotten her.

It's lovely when you can make a few people smile per day, comfort them and give them closure. That's what makes it all worthwhile. Just being there for people.

But it's not easy. I always knew it wasn't going to be easy, and it's not easy at all. You can be the best psychic in the world, but you cannot change what is coming. They choose us; we don't choose them.

Me with my eldest daughter Charmaine, 1981

My Nanna Ellen

My son Martin, daughter Charmaine, brother Chris, son Ashley,
daughter Joanne, daughter Katy

My daughter Joanne and son Ashley

My daughter Demi, daughter Joanne, grandson Nathan, and sons Little Jack and Ashley

Little Jack

My mother Pauline, me and grandson Nathan

Daughter Joanne, daughter Katy, mother Pauline, me, daughter Charmaine and daughter Demi

My son Martin

6

BABY JOHN

From the very minute my bouncing fourth baby was placed in my arms by the midwife at Jimmy's, I knew instinctively that he was special.

"You've been here before," I'd coo to him. "Probably multiple times." There was just something different about him.

Pale and fair with big blue eyes and huge hands for a baby, John, my second son, was the biggest of all my eight children, weighing in at a strapping 8lb 10oz on 2nd February 1986.

After my traumatic pregnancy with Katy, when I'd bled the whole way through, this one had been a breeze. I'd literally sailed through it. It was the same with the labour and, here he was, a picture of health. Everybody commented on it.

Naturally, it suited Martin's macho image to have another son. He'd always wanted a gang of boys. And, as young as they were, Charmaine, Martin and Katy absolutely worshipped their little brother. He was such a lovely, happy little baby, it was impossible not to.

But within days of his arrival, I just had a strong gut feeling that all was not what it seemed. I have never been able to 'read' for myself. I don't know any spiritual mediums who can: it's impossible. Even now, if I ask my Star People, "Is this or that going to happen?" they don't always tell me.

"Wait and find out for yourself," is the answer I often get.

Yet, strangely, I knew for certain that John was not going to be on this Earth plane for very long. So too did my mum. She always had a fear for little John. And, without giving too much away, my Star People confirmed my instinct this time. "Hold on to him, Paula. He's not going to be here for long," they began to warn me.

So, as my feeling grew deeper and deeper, I treasured my gorgeous little boy with the beautiful angelic smile while I could. He would look at me and I'd look at him as he sucked on his bottle, knowing we'd been together before.

I can still picture him in the kitchen in the high chair somebody had acquired from McDonalds, with the brown picture of Ronald McDonald on. He'd kick his little legs and wave his arms in excitement for the next spoonful of baby food that was coming his way. His absolute favourite was Heinz chocolate pudding!

The day he died, only six months old, on 7th August 1986, I felt like curling up and dying with him. I was devastated and numb with shock and grief. Absolutely devastated; absolutely numb.

It was 6am on a midweek morning when he woke up in

his purple carry cot, which sat at the side of my bed. It was a really sunny day, I remember that. I fed him his bottle and tickled him to make him chuckle.

Checking on him soon afterwards, I was horrified to find my lovely John turning stiff and blue. I screamed for Martin; he leapt into action and tried to give him the kiss of life while I ran out onto the street in just my bra and knickers, shouting for help. A lovely Irish lady came in and called an ambulance, which arrived and took him away.

When the funeral director phoned to tell me that my son was available for viewing in the chapel of rest, I decided not to go. I knew it wasn't really my John lying in there. My mum went with Martin, but I got two very different replies when I asked them individually to tell me what he'd looked like.

"He looked lovely, Paula. He looked fine. He really did," Martin reassured me.

My mum wasn't quite so sympathetic to my feelings, and told me he didn't even look like John – that he was 'black, like something out of a horror story.' I've had to wrestle with that image all my life.

Later, she had the cheek to say, "I believe that God has looked down on you because you had too much going on in your life, and has taken one child from you to be an angel."

Believe me, it was no comfort after the picture she'd painted of my little man. I didn't even have any photographs of him. At some point amongst all the trauma, a female coroner came to the house to ask me some questions. When the results of the post mortem came through, she ruled that it was 'Sudden Infant Death Syndrome.' A classic cot death. Despite a few vile accusations that were cast my way, it was not my fault.

Afterwards we built a fire in the garden. I burnt everything that had belonged to him: his little booties and cotton nighties. I burnt the lot; I didn't even save one item. After a little funeral service at Lawnswood Crematorium, his ashes were scattered in the rose garden with his Great-Grandma Mary.

Deep down, I knew that John had never really left me. Even though for a long time he stayed in the background, I could always sense him around, often smelling of baby milk. Once, he even came back to the living room where he'd passed away in Wykebeck Avenue, but it was as a column of light or energy. Suddenly the back door banged and he came in to lay on the sofa with me, our legs entwined. It was his first visit and it was fantastic. I was over the moon.

Some babies stay babies when they've passed; others grow in spirit. I've no idea why that is but it's a fact. John has grown in spirit and is now a man in his 30s. I'd say he's a cross between Ashley and Martin in looks. He's as tall as Ashley but stockier in build.

I know that because today, he's one of my doorkeepers – my protectors – and he has been for the past eight or 10 years. He's brilliant at seances, when I can ask him to tap tunes on the table. The guy filming us for a TV documentary about my psychic abilities was blown away when he witnessed that a few years ago.

I don't think, looking back, that I grieved properly for John. My main concern had to be for my other children. They were my priority, so I told them that John was in Heaven and put up a protective shield. Above all else, I had to shield them from my own grief. Especially because after his passing, my Star People had warned me, "There's one more to go…"

7

LIFE GOES ON

Newly wed and standing together outside Leeds Registry Office, Martin and I at least looked like a proper couple in our matching grey suits and white shirts. Once again I had a plain gold band on the third finger of my left hand. I was not heavily pregnant for my second wedding, unlike my first.

The civil ceremony took place not long after John died, and it was a quick affair. Afterwards we had a reception of sorts in a local pub. Just a few sandwiches with very close family members. I was officially his possession now. His trophy.

Soon after we'd lost John, Martin had wanted another baby. Another boy. It wasn't really a matter of what I wanted. Any romantic feelings we had for each other had now gone, but we still had sex. Sex was sex as far as I was concerned. Being obviously very fertile, I soon fell pregnant again.

In December 1987, with the sound of carols echoing all around the hospital, I was back in Jimmy's giving birth for the fifth time to Joanne. Our first child born in wedlock. It was a lovely festive atmosphere at the hospital, and it was a quick birth for an 8lb 2oz baby.

With her dark hair, little flat nose and narrow eyes, Joanne was the double of Martin. But it didn't make him happy. He was devastated not to have another boy.

Although my Star People's warning that I'd lose another child was still ringing in my ears, I didn't feel that it would be Joanne I lost. Like all my others, she was a good baby. Life was far from perfect but there was no way I could possibly leave Martin. It was fear, not love, keeping me there.

"Hang on, be strong," my Star People kept telling me. "We can't interfere, but you will always be strong of spirit, sound of mind.". I had to believe them, but I was very weary by this stage. Constantly exhausted, I even stopped doing readings for people. It wasn't so much a conscious decision; it just happened gradually as I hid myself away more and more.

Still Martin craved more boys, and I was obviously a baby making machine so I was back in Jimmy's again on 16th June 1989, having my sixth baby: a 7lb 7oz boy! So why wasn't Martin happy?

Because the new baby was dark haired and quite dark skinned, Martin didn't believe he was his child and accused me of sleeping with somebody else. Believe me, that was the last thing on my mind at that time.

When we eventually got round to naming him a fortnight later, Martin agreed with my choice of Ashley but it's true to say that they never really bonded, and today there's no communication whatsoever between them. It's Martin's loss and the irony is that Ashley is the double of his father, though only physically.

Ashley is very, very protective of me and the two of us are extremely close now. Maybe the bond between us is stronger because he hasn't got one with his father, but who can really say? It could also be because I always felt, from his early days, that Ashley would be the one I lost. It was a feeling that I carried throughout my life until fate decided what the next tragedy in my life should be… As I said, you can't read yourself, though I did start to read other people again. Often I would pass someone in the street and would need to tell them things. "A silver vehicle is going to crash…" Things like that. People got used to my warnings, which often came to me in dreams. I didn't charge for it: despite everything, Martin always looked after us financially. As I have said, he was a good provider like my father. Once he turned up with a metallic gold BMW 7 series saloon for me to learn to drive in so that I could ferry the kids about.

As they got older, Martin began to disappear on 'holidays' for a week or two at a time. It was no real surprise when I found a phone number in the pocket of his trousers and that, when I rang it, it was answered by a woman. Arranging to meet her, I learned that she was in the early stages of pregnancy. God bless her.

She helped me pack all Martin's stuff up and move it into her home. The kids and I all celebrated with chocolates and videos. They were ecstatic that he'd left! Over the moon! We all were.

Later he took our son Martin with him and, not wanting him in the middle of a tug of war, I didn't object. Initially there was a period of to-ing and fro-ing backwards and forwards like a yo-yo from one house to another, and within months of Martin's girlfriend giving birth to another of his sons, I was pregnant by him as well. Demi was born blue with the cord round her neck three or four weeks prematurely, on 22nd July 1995. In spite of my domestic situation, I can honestly say that she was the best thing that ever happened to me. All 5lb 9oz of her. Coming home from hospital with her is a lovely, lovely, memory. Her older siblings were all absolutely fascinated by this tiny little baby placed inside a Moses basket. They all just crowded around her and looked at her. We all adored her, with her masses of curls, but Katy in particular was absolutely besotted. She couldn't get over how gorgeous she was. She used to lift the blanket up at the bottom and just look at her feet.

"Look, Mum," she'd say, all excited. "Her feet remind me of ravioli!" Her little toes were just so perfect and tiny. So chubby as well.

The house was in uproar when Demi made an entrance. I can picture it now and it's a fantastic memory.

As we were fast outgrowing the three-bed place we were living in, Martin moved us into a five-bed semi. I'd passed my test by then and now had a smart white VW Calibra as well. I admit I was a bit naive about where the money was coming from. In January 2004, Martin was jailed for three years at Leeds Crown Court for supplying the class A drug ecstasy.

By then, we'd been divorced for three or four years, his girlfriend having insisted on it. He'd just turned up one day and told me to sign some papers, which I quite happily did. So, what with me being a 34-year-old mother of six living children, with an ex-husband like Martin, you could argue that I wasn't exactly the best catch for a 25-year-old man still living at home with his mum…

Me and daughter Demi

My daughter Demi

My daughters Demi and Joanne

Me, daughter Demi and daughter Katy

Me and daughter Demi

8

IT WASN'T ALL BAD

Despite all the ups and downs that I was encountering in my life, it's true to say that it wasn't all bad all of the time. After all, I did manage to produce a whole brood of beautiful children, who brought me such happiness.

Where do I even start trying to describe the fantastic memories I have of them all growing up? Left alone with them all, I was like a child myself. I just became one of them. They ran wild having fun and I ran wild having fun with them!

On the nights that Martin went out clubbing or partying all suited and booted – which he did quite a lot – we couldn't wait until he was out of the house. We were always delighted. Buzzing! I remember looking out of the window, with maybe Katy or Ashley beside me, watching him drive away up Osmondthorpe Lane. Out for the night, or maybe two or three or four nights. That was when our fun began!

I absolutely loved that time with my children, being on my own with them. I felt completely free. I could just be a mother to them. At this point there'd have been just the five:

Charmaine, Martin, Katy, Joanne and Ashley. As soon as he'd gone, we would gather together loads of crisps, sweets and chocolate, along with a children's magazine I used to buy them that came with a musical story tape. I'd head off first into my bedroom and they'd all follow me in. They were like little ducklings waddling along behind me! I'd climb into bed and they'd all make up their own individual little beds on the floor by the side of me, waiting for me to read the magazine and play the tape to them. We'd all sit and listen to it while munching our way through the 'tuck'. Sometimes we would watch videos together too. It was magical.

Birthdays were another special time. I always made sure they each had a party for their birthday, even if their dad didn't always approve. The one that sticks out most in my mind for some reason is Demi's birthday, when she was two or three. They were all there helping me to bake and ice a batch of buns, although they probably ate a quarter of the mixture out of the bowl! We made a trifle and little sandwiches too – just kids' sandwiches, ham or potted meat fillings – and there were bowls of crisps hanging around. You could guarantee that if there was a party, my mum was always there as well. She'd usually buy a birthday cake for them. It's strange. My mum was absolutely brilliant with my children; it was just me that she had the agenda with.

Easters were fun too, from the minute I walked into the house with a big black bin liner crammed with Easter eggs. The bin liner was supposed to hide them so that they'd be a surprise for Easter Sunday, but nobody was really fooled. They knew exactly what was inside! Sometimes, though, I would pinch one or two and end up eating them myself before the day, so that I had to go out and buy more. All kids love chocolate and sweets, but my kids saw Easter as something special. They used to get so excited and so giddy. I always made them a lovely big roast lamb dinner with a dessert every Easter Sunday, and there'd always be one of them hanging round me in the kitchen when I was making the gravy to go with it. Gravies are my speciality. My secret ingredient? Lots of love! You've got to enjoy making it. I also use a lot of herbs, usually – mint if it's for lamb; mixed herbs and bay leaves for stews. I've never used salt, ever. I just have my own little recipes, tried and tested over the years. Anything I see lying around goes in the pot. I've always cooked traditional food for the family. Back then, I even made my own Cornish pasties and steak pies: without a rolling pin to my name, I had to improvise and roll out the pastry with a milk bottle.

The kids still remember my home-cooked food now. They devoured it, even though at one stage Ashley had his own funny little quirk when it came to eating. For a time, when he was four or five years old, he was quite troubled and just wouldn't eat his food. He would only eat it off my plate, and would always run up and grab something off it, whatever it was – a sausage or a fish finger – and do a runner with it. I could never get him to eat from his own plate. His dad didn't really like it and I used to say, "Ashley! Naughty boy!

You can't do that. That's your dinner; this is mine." But he'd just laugh. I'm sure he knew what he was doing but he just wouldn't eat his own food, and I had to take the view that as long as he ate, that was the most important thing. He was the only one like that. Maybe he was a bit more sensitive than the others, I don't know. Nevertheless, they all grew up knowing how to cook themselves. Ashley and Katy in particular are still good cooks, and Demi can look after herself. She's more of a baker though, that's what she loves turning her hand to.

Like in most families, Christmas was another wonderful time for creating happy memories. You can imagine, having so many children, how many presents there were to be bought and wrapped. Loads!

About a week before Christmas Day, I used to go into town shopping by bus and come home with five or six bin liners full of toys, all to be wrapped and put under the lovely big Christmas tree that we always had in the living room. Often, during the big run up, I'd be sitting downstairs frantically wrapping them all while the children played upstairs. Charmaine, being the eldest, was my helper.

Her special job was to act as the doorkeeper, making sure that nobody (most likely Ashley) opened it and tried to have a peep inside the room to see what they were getting. You could bet your bottom dollar that one or two of the parcels would be ripped open before they were supposed to be. It was around this time that I started our family tradition of allowing them all to open one present on Christmas Eve. Of course they all wanted to rip into their present at the same time together, but purely for my own excitement I made them do it one at a time. From the eldest down to the youngest. I wanted to prolong it and savour every moment of seeing their happy, excited little faces and thought that if they all did it at once, it would be over too quickly! It was a lovely little tradition. I continued it for years and years.

Of course they used to fight amongst themselves as well. In lumps! There was a rumpus going off nearly every day. We had a pigeon loft in the back garden and my son Martin loved his pigeons – he still does to this day. One day though, unbeknown to me, Katy and Ashley had had a really bad argument so she'd marched up to the pigeon loft and let them all out with full bellies. Ashley was still walking back from school when he spotted a flock of pigeons in the sky above our house and thought, *Oh no!* He knew there was trouble ahead. There were at least a dozen of them, but fortunately they all came back home. I did manage to see the funny side of Katy's prank, but I had to stand between them both to stop a ferocious scrap kicking off when Ashley got in!

Another time, I was busy and didn't take much notice when Katy asked me, "Mummy, can I paint a penny on your bedroom door?"

"A penny? Well no, not really," I replied. "Why would you want to paint a penny anyway?"

She begged, "Oh please, please!" Any one of them had only to look at me like that and I'd give in, so I said, "Yes, all right, but your dad won't like it. Just don't make it too big."

As she went ahead and painted a pink circle with a penny in the middle, she announced, "I'm going to be a millionaire when I'm older."

Puzzled, I said, "Are you, Katy? Why, what are you going to do?"

"Well for now, if anybody wants to go into your bedroom I am going to charge them a penny, and I am going to make loads and loads of money doing that. That's what I wanted the penny on the door for."

I had to laugh and admire her for being so entrepreneurial. But soon her older sister Charmaine twigged onto this and found a stash of her dad's money – bang on £200 in £20 notes – and took it into the garden. After tearing up the notes, she buried – or 'planted' – them. When questioned, she said, "Look what I've done, Mum. I've ripped all the money up into little pieces because it makes it more, and it will grow into lots more £20 notes!" She must have been about seven or eight years old at the time and had heard the saying 'money grows on trees.' The result was £200 lost! She was lucky to escape any repercussion. Even Martin saw the funny side of it.

Although we never went away on holiday, we often went out together for walks round Temple Newsam or Roundhay Park with a picnic. In truth, all I ever wanted was for them to have the childhood I never had. I wanted to give them happy memories. Very different ones to my own.

As any loving mother knows, as much as you might want to, you cannot scatter rose petals in your children's path through life. You just have to do the best you can in the circumstances. Today, I don't see all my living children or their children, but I do have an exceptionally close relationship with the ones I do see, so I suppose I must have done something right! But please don't just take my word for it. Read what Katy and Ashley have to say.

Katy

If I am completely honest, I don't have a lot of memories from when I was young. I think I've blocked a lot out up to the age of 12. But I do remember living in a very busy household. It certainly wasn't a quiet home. Obviously, with so many siblings, there was always chaos going on. You learned pretty early on to get to the dinner table on time because, if you didn't, you missed all the good bits!

Growing up, I was a tomboy who used to play football – not for a team, just with the boys. It's true to say that I was actually a better player than my big brother Martin, and he really didn't like that. Especially when I tried to show him up in front of his mates! I was a little brat sometimes. If I did lose at football, I'd let his pigeons out. He'd see them from the football field and he'd have to race home.

There were quite a few happy times but there were more sad times, though the sad times weren't down to my mum. When Demi arrived, we were going through a very turbulent time in the house. None of it was my mum's fault but I felt very alone at that point. Demi changed the whole dynamic of the house. It was like a new lease of life. She and I bonded straight away. We were a team. I used to take her everywhere with me, and we've kept that bond all our lives even though we don't see each other that much now I am living in New Zealand.

My mum's right when she says that she became one of us when my dad wasn't there. Home was a really nice place to be then. She would cook us all these amazing meals. I remember peeling a lot of spuds when I was younger. My nickname was Spud, or Katy Potaty! And I loved her gravy. I still do. It's like soup!

Once she came up with a points system for us kids to try and make us all behave. If we did a good deed like wash the dishes, we could earn some points, which were written down in a scorebook. Whoever had the most points at the end of the week got a present, like a day out or a trip to Uncle Chris's. It was always a real treat to go there because we'd always play games and get sweets. I found out where Mum had hidden the scorebook and I added some points onto my score. That's why I always won! It lasted about six months, I think.

Another time, when I was about 10, I remember Mum, Dad and Dad's friend calling me into the living room and telling me to put my hand in a black velvet bag filled with gold jewellery. Whatever I picked out, I could have. I got a massive ring, but I think I swapped it for something else. It wasn't an ordinary childhood!

Despite everything, Mum always looked really lovely and once I remember rooting round her make up drawer and finding a pair of beautiful diamond earrings. She had lovely stilettos as well, which I put on even though they were far too big for me. It was late one afternoon and the house was unusually quiet, but Mum came into her bedroom and caught me red handed jumping on her nicely made double bed wearing the shoes and earrings!

Most of the time when my dad was there though you had to watch what you were doing and saying. You had to be very careful. It felt like a lot of the time we just had to 'make do' and I don't think we ever realised the value of money until we got much older. Sometimes we seemed to have it in extremes, and then it would just go. But that wasn't my mum's fault either. She just tried to bring up her kids and do the best she could do at the time. She was dealt a really bad hand at a very young age.

I think the day my dad left, we all actually celebrated! I remember Mum going out and buying loads of sweets and chocolate and us all sitting around smiling. It felt like a nice family home. And when we did have happy times, we remembered them forever. I will always remember sitting on the sofa watching Christmas carols being sung on the telly and eating loads of lovely food. Christmas was always a lovely time. I don't actually ever remember my dad being there at Christmas. I do remember Uncle Freddie being there though, even though I didn't really know what relation he was to our family for years. I've since learnt that he was my dad's mum's then-husband's brother. To put it a bit simpler, he was my Granddad Peter's brother, who brought his own stories and his own energy and life and a bit of cheek into our house, where he would lodge from time to time. When I was a little girl I was always kind of scared of Freddie, who worked as a street trader in Leeds. He was a jack of all trades and a real character. I wasn't scared of him in a bad way; being young, I just didn't understand him. For me Freddie was an old, hairy, wrinkly guy. He never really got involved in playing with us – he wasn't that kind of person. You never got a lot out of him, but when he did say something you would listen. A lot of the time it felt as if you were getting told off by him, but he always had my mum's back covered. He used to stick up for her, and she needed all the friends and supporters that she could get.

I will always treasure the happy memories she created whenever she had the opportunity but, in truth, they were very few and far between.

Ashley

Despite everything, Mum always had a good sense of humour and it passed on to all her children. You had to see the funny side of stuff growing up in our house.

Looking back, there are loads of funny memories – like when we'd mimic Ant and Dec's Royal Rumbles on their PJ and Duncan show. We'd basically all dive on top of each other on the bed and fight! It always ended up with me on the bottom, stuck because I was the smallest! Charmaine was the biggest and she always won.

Once, I remember being so worried about being small because a school friend was taller than me. I asked my mum and dad's friend Charlie why that was, and he said, "Haven't your mum and dad told you yet? It's because you're a dwarf!"

I ran off crying to my mum. "Charlie's just told me I'm a wharf!" She went along with it until she realised just how upset I was! It always amused her when we thought daft things like that. It was the same the time Katy ate the pips in her apple and was so worried about what would happen to her that she asked Uncle Chris for his advice on the matter. Playful and dramatic, he said, "Oooh! You know a tree's going to grow out of your head." She was in tears until Mum stopped seeing the funny side and put her right.

As well as having a good sense of humour, I remember that Mum always looked really glamorous. Even when she was just at home, she always made sure she looked her best. I can still smell her perfume, which was usually Chanel No 5 or 19.

That didn't mean she wasn't a hands-on type of mother, though. I remember coming home from school sometimes or waking up in the morning and there'd be rabbits or pheasants in bin liners that my dad's friends had left on the doorstep. It was always left to Mum to clean and gut them. As kids we were fascinated to see her skinning rabbits, but she'd shout at us to get out of the kitchen. We'd be knocking on the door asking, "Can we come in yet?"

She was always in the kitchen preparing or cooking and food was a massive thing for us. She'd make great meals with lots of gravies, sausages, game pies, pork pies. We always had a lot of meat.

Growing up, Joanne and I were really close. Wherever she was, I was and vice versa. We were best friends, like Katy and Martin were. The four of us would take the 91 bus home and race down Osmondthorpe Lane on the day we got our school reports to see who could be the first to get theirs to Mum and Dad. If it was a good report we'd get a prize. I was a goody two shoes back then, and one year I got a day out to Flamingo Land, a theme park and zoo in North Yorkshire. I remember that fondly. If your report wasn't good, though, you'd get a clip round the ear! I wasn't quite so good when I hit my teens: I rebelled a bit because of the situation at home. I think we all rebelled to an extent. But it certainly isn't any reflection on my mum.

She wasn't a soft touch by any means. One morning, Katy didn't want to go to school and threw vinegar all over her white school shirt so that she couldn't go. But Mum sent her anyway, stinking of vinegar. That was a lesson learned.

The happiest times were definitely when my dad wasn't around. Mum would get us all round the telly, but first she'd give Katy and me 20 quid and send us on our little pushbikes to the top shop to buy loads of sweets. Once I think we bought about 1,000 penny sweets. The shopkeeper must have cursed us.

I do remember one occasion when my mum and dad had been out together. When they came back in they put all these bin liners in the middle of the room and said, "Go on kids, jump in!" It wasn't Christmas or anyone's birthday; I don't know what it was. There were all these toys, every kind of toy you could think of. Everything from colouring books to a little bingo set. Toys upon toys upon toys. I remember it really clearly.

One very hot summer, I found my mum's matches. My dad had been out and they must have been changing the beds or ordered new mattresses. There was a mattress in the back garden that we used to jump off the garage roof onto. The garden was on a slope, so it wasn't as far to fall as it sounds. However, it wasn't so safe when I dropped a match onto it. Whoosh! The whole garden went up in flames: the shed, the garage. We were lucky not to lose the house as well. That didn't go down too well with Mum, I can tell you.

If I'm honest, I think I've blocked out the bad memories from my childhood. It probably helps that I was only seven when Mum and Dad split up. Katy was older. As a result, I have more fond memories. And thanks to Mum, there are loads of those.

My grandson Nathan, daughter Katy, daughter Joanne and son Ashley

Grandson Nathan and son Ashley

Little Jack, daughter Katy, grandson Nathan, daughter Charmaine, daughter Demi

My daughter Demi, daughter Charmaine, me and daughter Katy

My daughter Demi, my husband Jack and our son Little Jack

Me, my daughter Katy and son Ashley

My sons Little Jack and Ashley

*My daughter Katy, husband Jack, me, Ashleys partner Kyle, daughter Demi and son Ashley.
Christmas 2016*

9

SOULMATES

Striding into my best friend's mum's house to deliver a pile of ironing, I cheekily asked, "So who's Jack?"

It was around November time in 1998 and I knew full well who Jack Bairstow was. He was the reason I was there in the first place.

In the background, The Verve was playing – 'Sonnet', of all tracks!

"Yes, there's love if you want it…" go the lyrics. And one look at Jack, my pal Janet's younger brother, was enough. I knew instinctively that I would marry him and have a son. The moment I saw him in that living room I instantly knew that we were soulmates. I would marry him and we'd have a child together. I knew it, I just knew. Beyond all doubt.

He looked at me, grinned and answered, "I'm Jack," as I nearly tripped over in my excitement to hand over the designer gear he paid Janet to wash and iron for him.

"Are you all right, love?" he asked, all concerned. Apart from feeling a bit of a clumsy fool, I was absolutely fine.

Back in those days, without sounding as if I'm bragging, it's true to say that I could have my pick of guys. Another husband and baby had been the last thing on my mind before I had walked into that house on an 'errand' for Janet. Really it was just part of a plot we'd hatched so that I could meet the man that Janet's teenage daughter told me I reminded her of. I'd simply been intrigued.

I'd known Janet for years. We'd met when we were both standing outside the gates of Whitebridge Primary School at Halton Moor waiting for our kids to come out. We started having a chinwag and became good pals, but we'd lost touch after a couple of years.

We'd bumped into each other again when I got into keeping fit and was running four miles a day round the historic Temple Newsam estate. A Tudor Jacobean mansion, it's famous for its grounds, which were landscaped by the man dubbed 'England's Greatest Gardener', Capability Brown. Today, hundreds of women follow in my footsteps every year to do the Cancer Research UK Race for Life. Janet's mum didn't live far from there and neither did mine.

By this time, Janet was a single mum like me and was earning a few extra quid by helping out her brother. One with a liking for immaculately laundered designer clothes like the ones I was delivering to him. Labels like Lacoste and Henri Lloyd didn't come cheap and must have taken a big dent out of his semi-skilled engineer's wages.

I'd heard a lot about Jack from Janet. We were good pals

and we looked after each other. On Friday or Saturday nights, we'd taken to having a couple of glasses of rose wine at her house and playing 1960s music or songs from the popular film *Dirty Dancing* with Patrick Swayze. Sometimes I'd take Demi with me.

According to Janet's daughter, Jack was into keeping fit, like me, and was lovely looking with the bluest of eyes. She made him sound like a film star and I wasn't disappointed when I saw him. Nor he with me, it seemed. It was obvious to both of us that there was an instant attraction. Probably to his mother too, who, like his brother Peter, was eyeballing me.

Be calm, be calm, I kept telling myself. He was a lot younger than me and only just about ready to fly the nest. It would take a brave man to take me and all my baggage on.

Nevertheless, I was already hooked and the first place I headed after my 'errand' was to Janet's to report back. "Wow! He's absolutely gorgeous, isn't he?"

Further enquiries revealed that he was single and that we were both Virgos, whose characteristics include loyalty and kindness. Our birthdays were a day apart, Jack's on 16th September and mine on 17th. A good omen? Soulmates? I like to think so.

Conscious of the fact I was born in 1964 and he was born in 1973, I was determined not to push anything – even though Janet thought we were like two peas in a pod. I found myself round at Jack's house once again around teatime on Christmas Eve, after he invited me to pop in for a Christmas drink and a bite to eat with Charmaine, who was probably about 16 at the time. She was all glammed up with perfect hair and make up, but I didn't bother dressing up. I just went as I was. Jack was probably drinking wine, but I was driving. I've never been much of a drinker myself (I don't touch alcohol today), so I just stuck to lemonade. It didn't stop me having a good laugh with him, but I did feel a bit nervous when we had a little boogie about to the music. Mostly, though, we just sat next to each other on his mum's sofa chatting. We could chat about anything and everything – my kids, my soon-to-be ex-husband, how strange it was that our mums lived next door but one to each other. Just general chit chat, but we got on so, so, so well. The rapport between us was unbelievable. Just brilliant.

I can remember getting up to go to the toilet and that when I came back into the living room, Charmaine was sitting in my space in the middle of the sofa. I sat down at the opposite end to Jack, leaving her in the middle, and he moved round to me and asked her to move up.

"He's an absolute peach isn't he, Mum?" I can remember Charmaine saying numerous times. He was! It was a lovely, lovely night. As I started making tracks to go home, Jack asked, "Which of you is going to give me a kiss, then?"

I stayed sitting where I was, but Charmaine jumped up to kiss him. I said, "It takes a lot, lot more than that for me to give you a kiss, Jack!" I suppose I was playing a bit hard to get.

Another Saturday night, not so long afterwards, I was

round at Janet's house when Jack called in for a few drinks. Back in those days, he was seriously into fitness and could run 20 miles without a struggle. For fun! How we age! Not surprisingly, he had an enviable six pack and looked lovely in a crisp white shirt and a pair of jeans with a thick leather Armani belt. The song *Hungry Eyes* from the Dirty Dancing soundtrack was playing as we whispered in each other's ears, our own eyes starving for each other. By the end of the night, I'd drunk too much wine to drive home and Jack offered me his single bed there. I didn't even undress when I got in, after phoning Charmaine to check that everything was OK at home.

Soon, though, I heard him come into the bedroom and whisper, "Paula?" Then, realising that I was awake, he asked, "Do you mind if I get into bed with you?"

Now for me to sleep with someone just like that was completely out of character. Normally I would have had to be in a full-blown relationship to take that step. But on this occasion I had no hesitation in saying yes and, ever the gentleman, he climbed in still wearing his designer jeans!

The next morning I woke up thinking, *What have I done? He's absolutely gorgeous and he could have his pick of women.* I felt as if I'd made a huge mistake getting involved. Yet something else inside me was thinking, *No, it's not a mistake.* And if I needed any further reassurance, my Star People were quick to agree with me.

Downstairs, Janet was grinning like a Cheshire cat but she warned me, "Paula, he's going to be hard to pin down. I know he thinks the world of you but I know our Jack…" She'd already told me he was one for the lasses.

Despite everything that was against us – and there was a lot – he sent me a dozen red roses on Valentine's Day and the rest, as they say, is history. Less than a year after that first meeting, on 18th October 1999, we were married at Hull Registry Office. We didn't have a penny to our name and it took a long time to scrape together the £50 or whatever it was that we needed to pay for a marriage license. I can remember us turning up for the ceremony together in a Peugeot 106. No superstition for us about the bride and groom not seeing each other on their wedding morning! Our lovely kind friends Jean – who, bless her, has sadly since passed away – and Alan threw a little reception for us at their house. We weren't even expecting a traditional wedding cake, but they borrowed one from somewhere so that we could pose with it for the photographs. We weren't allowed to cut or eat it though, and unfortunately we've since lost all the pictures. Jack still jokes today that it was the best cake we've ever had!

Within weeks of us getting together, I'd started to feel strange: sick, dizzy and off balance. I'd fallen pregnant. The only precaution we'd taken was to use the notoriously unreliable withdrawal method, but I was still shocked when I did a test and saw two blue lines. Within the hour I'd rung Jack at work with the news.

"OK, we'll deal with it. I'm over the moon to be a dad. I'm going to be a dad!" was his reaction.

There was no question about abortion, and he was genuinely thrilled to be a father for the first time. I had known it would happen from the moment I'd met him, and I knew he'd be pleased. Less so my ex-husband, I feared…

However, four or five days later, Jack had gone to work and I suddenly started bleeding really heavily, crippled with pain. Janet took me to the hospital, where I was examined and given an injection in the bum, as I had rhesus negative blood and could have developed antibodies that would attack the baby's blood cells. Despite obeying all orders to rest, I lost the baby. I think it was a little girl. I was devastated and so was Jack. But if I lay my cards on the table, I have to say that I knew in my heart of hearts that it wasn't the right time. We didn't even have a home together: I was still living in Martin's house despite the divorce. I couldn't see him letting Jack move in.

Another bombshell for Jack, which also occurred within weeks of us meeting and getting together, was my shock confession of my childhood abuse. I didn't want any secrets, so I laid everything bare. He went very quiet as I told him all the gory details. Finally he asked me, "What did your mum do about it?" He cried when I answered, "Nothing." Then I cried, and I actually thought, *This is too much for him*. But he didn't try to run away. That came later, and I was with him. Demi came with us and Joanne and Ashley followed.

After my miscarriage, we headed for Scarborough to start afresh. I sold all the gold and diamond jewellery Martin had bought me and we survived a fortnight before heading for Hull.

Officially registered homeless, we ended up in a hostel for three months in a strange city.

We liked Hull at first, and its people – especially Alan and Jean, who soon became good friends to us. Eventually we got a council semi, where I fell pregnant again in April 1999. We both wanted another baby after the miscarriage, and we were aware that my biological clock was ticking away, so you could say it was planned. Despite our circumstances, I was elated by the news, as was Jack. I knew instinctively that I was having a boy even before the first scan.

'There's another Jack on the way," I told him happily, and that's when we made plans to get married very quietly and cheaply at the registry office. I still can't believe that I've been married three times and never worn a traditional white wedding dress!

Strangely, I never felt I would lose this baby, and I felt as fit as a fiddle throughout my pregnancy, even though I'd been warned by doctors after giving birth to Demi that another pregnancy could have a serious impact on my health. I wanted a baby with Jack so much that I ignored the advice. My Star People made sure I had a nice feeling throughout, constantly reassuring me.

Little Jack Anthony (who was almost Jack Alfie) arrived at Castlehill Hospital, Beverley, at 9.15am on 19th January 2000. My 5lb 8oz millennium baby! He should have been born at Heddon Road hospital in Hull, but the ambulance took me to the wrong hospital by mistake and my labour was too advanced to move me. I gave one mighty push and he was out. Katy was the first to hold him and Daddy Jack, who was holding my hand at the top end, cut the cord on this gorgeous tiny little red blonde thing with big blue eyes. Tears streamed down his face as he did it. He was totally mesmerised by his new son. Worryingly though, Little Jack (as he immediately became known) arrived shaking from head to foot, which I blame on the stress we were under at the time.

Certain family members back in Leeds were almost queuing up to tell me I'd made a huge mistake and that Jack, being nine years younger than me, would leave me the minute I'd had the baby. All I can say is that he's still here. My one true love. My soulmate.

We were having a really bad time in Hull and Jack was feeling the pressure. He'd tried a couple of jobs but nothing had worked out, so we were constantly penniless and trying to keep a roof over our heads and enough Kwik Save's budget-range food on the table. Jack's way of coping was to drink cheap beer, which was becoming a problem. We rowed, of course we did. We were on the point of destitution, and homesick for Leeds. I did a few readings for neighbours but it didn't bring in any money. The house we were living in was damp and full of ants and mice. A mouse even ran over Katy's bed. It wasn't good for baby Jack's health – or for the health of the rest of us, either. Despite being a smoker, I knew that the cough, cough, cough habit I developed there was nothing to do with cigarettes. The stabbing pains in my back were literally doubling me over, and I couldn't breathe. I knew I was really ill so I called a doctor out to visit me at the house. He diagnosed water on my lungs and prescribed me with antibiotics; they did the job of making me better, but they were so strong that they knocked me completely off my feet at the same time. Looking back, I think my immune system must have been very, very low at the time. I suppose it was no surprise really, given the poor conditions we were all living in.

To be fair to my mum, for all her faults she knew the kids were having it tough and she had a word with my dad. He stumped up £1500 so that we could move back to Leeds and have enough to pay six months' rent up front on a privately owned townhouse on the west side of the city. Plus proper food for the kids. I didn't want to accept it – it put me back where he wanted me: dependent on him. At that time, though, I had no choice but to accept. I was in a no-win situation.

The first time he met Jack – and was reunited with me again – he looked at us both and had tears rolling down his face. "Why did you do what you did to me?" I wanted to ask him. "You could have been such a spot-on father."

Settled back in Leeds, Jack had a few engineering jobs but he struggled with his nerves, and Stella lager became his medication. Part of his problem was his inability to accept the way my father had treated me as a child. He just couldn't move on.

I didn't like being in my father's debt either, but my anxieties came out in different ways: panic attacks, claustrophobia and significant agoraphobia. I'd been suffering panic attacks on and off since my 20s, but when my old Peugeot broke down one night and I had to walk 10 minutes uphill back home, I was so terrified. I had a huge panic attack that I thought was going to kill me. Within days, doctors had diagnosed severe agoraphobia and told me that it was a direct result of the life I had lived.

Life was a constant struggle without enough money to live on and, panicked, I rang my dad. He promised, "I'll never see you without." He offered me £10,000 initially to tide me over, though the sum was eventually reduced to £8,000. I felt uncomfortable about taking it and knew there was something not quite right about the transaction, especially when one family member wanted me to sign a legal declaration that I'd received it. Absolutely not! No way! I stood my ground and refused point-blank to sign their agreement.

It turned out that the money wasn't being offered through love or even out of guilt, but out of fear of what I might do. He and my mum were scared that I'd take them to court over the abuse. Did my parents really think that £8,000 was enough compensation for what he'd inflicted on me? Was this the going rate for robbing me of my childhood?

"I'll f***ing bury you in court," he told me on the phone one night, and something clicked in my head. Anger kicked in, and I went into fight mode.

"Right then, bring it on," I answered him.

"Bring it f***ing on. How dare you after how good your

mother's been to your children? It's all in your head," was his reply.

It was his arrogance and complete disregard for me that did it. I knew I couldn't have him talking to me like that after everything he'd put me through and I finally snapped. My mind was set.

On a cold, grey day that same week, I drove off to Seacroft, near the notorious Halton Moor estate, with Jack and Ashley. As we parked up, I knew what I had to do next. With my father's whispered mantra, *"It's our little secret,"* ringing in my ears, I walked through the glass doors of Killingbeck Police Station in May 2009. There was no going back now.

My husband Jack

10

JUSTICE IS DONE

'How can I help you?' asked the uniformed male officer on the reception desk.

"Where do I start?" I shrugged helplessly.

Despite everything I'd been put through, I was still heartbroken that it had come to this. I took no pleasure in what I was doing – in fact I felt very, very down about it all. But I knew I couldn't have my father talking to me like that. I didn't know what he and my mother were really saying about me behind my back, and I had a strong feeling they were cooking something up against me.

Years of overheard conversations between the two of them, which were always along the lines of, "Who's going to believe her?" had taken their toll. I half doubted myself that the police – or any jury – would believe me.

"Tell me why you're here," he urged.

So, taking a deep breath, I told him, "I want to report my father for raping me." There. I'd said it.

Realising my distress, the policeman asked, "Are you OK?"

before I was led into a small, white-walled, windowless room with four or five blue hard-backed chairs and a melamine table. In there, I met two female officers in plain clothes. One was quite young – in her 30s, I'd say – and the other was older, probably in her 50s. They made me a cup of tea and helped me to relax as much as I possibly could.

"Where do I even start with this?" I remember asking them. "As far back as you can remember," came the reply.

So that's exactly what I did. My sorry story started to come spilling out as they listened to the details of all the events and sexual activities that had gone on with my father. It was horrendous. I was crying and Jack, who was with me, bless him, was crying as well as he held my hand. I'd told all three of my husbands about the abuse, but Jack was the most supportive by far. 100 percent.

The elder of the two women had to stop me before I'd finished.

"It's far too complex, is this," she admitted. "We're going to get somebody else involved who's going to come to your house and interview you, Paula. Somebody who is trained to specialise in cases like this."

I must've been in there for a good hour just crying and talking, but the strange thing was that, despite my distress, it was just nice to have someone listen to me and not judge me. They didn't call me a liar. They sat and listened. I actually felt as if they believed me, believed that I wasn't making it up. It was common knowledge in the family, and with people who weren't even blood relatives, that Paula had been raped, but it had always been swept under the carpet. I'd always been told, "Nobody will listen to you. You're cuckoo. Who's going to believe that? Your dad is a businessman with two betting shops." I was known as the twisted sister and I suppose to an extent that will have been drilled into my mind.

Yet here I was, and here were these two officers being absolutely lovely to me, listening intently and taking me so seriously. That felt amazingly empowering, and made me realise, *I can do this*.

Walking out of that police station, I actually felt elated. I was still heartbroken, but so happy as well if that makes sense. It felt as if a huge weight had been lifted from my shoulders.

Jack said, "You've done it now. You've set the ball rolling. It's your choice, Paula, but do it for yourself to prove you're not cuckoo. I'll support you every single step of the way." Bless him.

Thankfully, Jack wasn't the only one to support me. I think it was the very next day that another plain clothes female officer, Kirsty Walsh, turned up on my doorstep with a male colleague. She was from a specialist team that dealt with historic abuse cases and I felt very comfortable with her right from the start. That feeling that somebody was listening to me and taking me seriously kept me going. And the more she listened, the more I talked.

At some point, she explained to me that I'd have to be filmed and that it would be shown to specialist voice analysts and body language experts. That didn't faze me in the slightest.

"What do I do? Do I smile?' I asked. "Just be yourself," she told me.

Over the next 18 months I saw a hell of a lot of Kirsty, answering all her questions about the intimacy between my father and me. Yes, it was embarrassing having to go into it all and I really, really struggled with it. But Kirsty was so professional; she was brilliant.

As well as questioning me, she had a lot to check out, including my medical records. From them she gleaned that, even though I still can't remember it, I'd told a GP when I was under 16 that I was being abused. It was on my medical notes, along with a record of all the prescriptions for the cream I'd needed 'for intimate use'. It was all there in black and white, yet nothing had ever been done about it.

Kirsty left no stone unturned, and the evidence was mounting against my mum and dad, but it was still a very anxious time waiting to find out whether charges were going to be brought against them by the Crown Prosecution Service. My dad's words about burying me if the case got to court went round and round in my head, along with numerous other threats that were made against me. Both my mum and my dad phoned me on a number of occasions before they were charged to scoff, "You haven't got a leg to stand on," and much, much worse.

"It's all just been for nothing. It's going to go the other way," I'd convince myself in my down moments.

It felt like such a long time, and even Kirsty's reassurances that there was so much investigative and preparation work to get through didn't really make me feel confident.

Only one of my four brothers had agreed to stand up and bear witness for the prosecution if it came to court, and that was Christopher.

Christopher was the one I'd begged to sleep with me in my single bed every Friday night. That was when, without fail, my dad, after a few drinks, would come round to visit after we'd moved. When my mum heard him come in, she'd get up out of her bed and tell Christopher to move out of mine to make way for my dad. One night he refused, and my dad dragged him out of the bed so that he could get in with me. So Christopher was a very important witness in the case.

I was pottering around in the kitchen when the landline phone rang sometime around the start of summer 2011. It was Kirsty, with news.

"Hi Paula, how are you feeling?" she asked.

"I'm struggling a bit now, Kirsty," I told her honestly. My agoraphobia and panic attacks were getting worse as the wait dragged on, and I was losing faith that the case would ever get to court.

"Well, it is going to court! The Crown Prosecution Service are going to prosecute!" Kirsty told me, and she started reading out all the charges against my mum and my dad.

My God! I became unsteady on my feet and to stop myself from collapsing, I had to sit down to listen to the catalogue of crime against their name: rape x number of times; indecent this, indecent that. And there were indecent assaults on others that I can't mention. The police tried for conspiracy charges but that didn't work, so my mum ended up being charged with neglect. I couldn't believe it.

"Any charge they could bring against your mum and dad, they have done," Kirsty told me. To be honest I don't think even Kirsty was expecting the CPS to hammer them both like that.

Completely shocked, I just burst into tears and told her, "Irrelevant of what happens at the end of all this, Kirsty, thank you so much for listening to me."

That was always the best thing about the case. In fact, before the jury even went out at Leeds Crown Court in July 2011, I asked the Judge (who I'm sure I called Mr Judge, I was so nervous) if I could just take a moment to thank him and the jury simply for listening to me.

I gave my evidence at the start of the trial via a video link, from a small room far away from the courtroom. Just the idea of entering the huge, imposing court building had been traumatic enough for me because of my agoraphobia. I'd had to know where I could park and how far I'd need to walk from the car. Knowing that the press and my mum, dad and brothers would be milling around, I was frightened that nerves would get the better of me and I would have a massive panic attack in front of everybody. I didn't want everybody laughing at me.

Luckily, Kirsty was able to make special arrangements for me to drive right up and slip in the back way, which was brilliant. I knew I was going to be questioned upside down but that I had to be strong. I will never ever forget how upset Jack got. As we arrived, he started sobbing and sobbing and sobbing, splashing great big tears on the floor. He was heartbroken by the lack of family support I had there. But I had him and Joanne by my side, and Ashley and Christopher somewhere nearby (though I couldn't be near them as they were both witnesses for the prosecution). I could do this.

Looking back, if I'd really had to stand in the dock in the main courtroom and face my parents to give evidence (as my dad tried to insist), I would have done. I'd come this far and nothing – but *nothing* – was going to stop me. Thankfully His Honourable Mr Justice Butterfield spared me that ordeal (and put my dad straight in his place) by saying that he was more than happy for me to stay where I was.

What a nice man he was! He even allowed me short breaks for water and cigarettes when it all got too much for me. I was questioned for what seemed like a lifetime. It was all so distressing. I was a nervous wreck. I cried a lot and I began to shake when I had to go into the horrific details in front of everyone. It was quite an ordeal and Jack couldn't stay in the room with me, but I knew he was sitting just outside in the corridor. Ultimately, though, I feared nothing because I knew that all I had to do was tell my story as it had really happened.

"Just tell the truth," the lovely female usher instructed me as she held my hand to settle me down and make me feel comfortable in front of the big TV screen. Oh, I fully intended to. I swore on the Bible that I would – even though I must admit that felt a bit funny, me being a witch. But at that point my old Catholicism kicked in, so I suppose you could say that I'm a sort of Catholic witch!

My Star People were the only people in the room with me, and they encouraged me throughout. "Continue, Paula. Don't stop," they kept repeating. "You're a survivor, not a victim."

When you're not lying you can't be tripped up. And not even the defence barristers, who my father had warned would 'chew me up and spit me out', could trip me up with their questions. The same cannot be said of my mum and dad, who both pleaded not guilty to all charges but dug themselves into deeper and deeper holes when questioned separately by the tall prosecution barrister (who reminded me of a big bat in his wide, black robe).

I was not allowed to listen, but according to Jack and other family members my dad was asked if at any point he got into my bed when I was a young girl. He admitted that yes, it was possible that he did when he was drunk.

When my mum took the stand and was asked if at any point she had let her ex-husband get into my bed with me, she started laughing and answered, "Absolutely not." According to her, whenever he came to our house he stayed on the sofa. Not only did it contradict my dad's evidence (given when she was outside the courtroom), but it also contradicted my brother Chris's, who backed up my evidence about what really went on in my bedroom.

During my questioning, I just told it exactly as it was. When asked why I sent my dad Christmas cards telling him I loved him, I told how I'd been trained all my life to think that what he was doing was normal. That it was the thing to do to keep my dad and my family happy, but that I'd also grown to understand how desperately depraved it was, how wrong. When told how strange it was that I trusted my mum to look after my children, I explained that I knew she would not harm a hair on their heads and that she knew I was in an abusive relationship.

"No further questions," the defence announced, quite abruptly, and I breathed a sigh of relief. My ordeal was over, and I'd survived it. Whatever the final outcome, I'd told the truth, the whole truth and nothing but the truth.

I never went back to court after giving my evidence. Jack did, but I stayed away and was actually at a filling station putting petrol in my car when I received the news that I'd won my court battle. My Star People, who I've never had any cause to doubt, had told me that I'd won after the jury had gone out. But it was a phone call from one of my cousins that officially confirmed it first (quickly followed by calls from Jack and Kirsty).

All I heard were the words, "Your dad's been convicted of raping you," before I dropped the phone and fell to the floor. Ashley had to get out of the car and pick me up.

"I can't believe they believed me," I told him. "Why wouldn't they believe you, Mum?" he asked.

When nobody ever has, though, it is a shock when they do. I can still remember one occasion years back – probably when I was in my 20s or 30s – when my dad turned round to my mother and my brothers and in a rare moment of honesty admitted, "Paula's not twisted. She's telling the truth. It's not Paula's fault, it's my fault."

Yet my brothers thought I'd put him up to it. My mother's words all those years before had not been wasted: "You know Paula: she's got her dad twisted round her little finger…"

This time, though, I was believed. I was listened to. And it was such a good feeling.

As Judge Butterfield told them when sentencing them, "You are both responsible for causing her serious psychological damage. The offences took place in Paula's own home. That was perhaps the one place in the whole world where she should have been protected from harm. But it was the one place in the whole world where she was caused terrible harm.

"Week after week, month after month, year after year. Between you, you destroyed that little child and you have affected the whole of her life."

He told my mother, "Not only did you stop your ears to the cries for help from your little daughter, but you allowed your former husband to visit your home, knowing perfectly well what he would do."

At 67, my father, Joseph Joyce, was found guilty of two

offences of rape and five other indecency charges against me, and sentenced to 12 years in prison. He was also found guilty of five further indecency charges relating to two other female victims.

My mother, who had remarried and was now Pauline Bennett, received a four-year sentence for child neglect and indecent assault on a teenager.

Wow. I was physically and mentally exhausted and I can't honestly say the verdict gave me any real peace. I didn't love either of my parents, but I did pity them. I can't remember exactly when it was – maybe when I was in my mid-20s – but my father had once told me that he was an abuse victim himself, which just makes me feel really sad. Extremely sad. And I was genuinely sad that it had all come to this. But on the other hand, what a relief! The whole country now knew from all the press coverage that Paula was not a liar, that she was not sick, that she was not the twisted sister, and that was really important to me. Justice had finally been done and I could start to move on and put it all behind me. About time too.

Me, 2015

Me, 2018

11

ALL THE VICTIM'S FAULT?

As a regular *Coronation Street* viewer, I've always quite liked William Roache, the distinguished actor who's played Ken Barlow ever since the first episode of the show was aired on 9th December, 1960. Before I was even born.

I not only admired his brilliant acting talent, but also the fact that he seemed a highly intelligent guy.

As well as being the longest serving living television actor in a continuous role, I'd read that he was a very spiritual person, which genuinely made me think that he was a man after my own heart. *What a nice guy! It's good to see someone of his age like that,* I thought. Not anymore.

Imagine my shock then when I opened a copy of the *Daily Star* newspaper and read his obnoxious, outspoken alleged views about abuse victims like me.

Apparently, he believes that we probably all deserve the abuse we get because of our own behaviour in past lives.

Oh really, Mr Roache? I spent 10 years being sexually abused by my father while my mother watched on. I was a young child. What could I have ever possibly done to deserve that? Do tell me, Mr Roache, because I cannot even begin to imagine for myself. What could one possibly do to deserve that? As a child, a young child?

To say that I was absolutely disgusted by his alleged remarks would be an understatement. I'm a firm believer in freedom of speech and that everybody is entitled to their own views – on reincarnation or otherwise – but I couldn't believe my eyes when I first read what he was reported to be saying. Then I couldn't carry on reading it anyway, because I was crying so much that I couldn't see the words on the page. It made me sob buckets to think that, in this enlightened day and age, people could still think like that. It 100 percent undermined me and upset me. Not just for myself but for the thousands upon thousands of others who have been in exactly the same situation. I won't have been the only one that his alleged comments reduced to tears for a couple of days.

I was truly shocked at what he was reported to have said; that somebody of his calibre, so to speak, could apparently come out with a tongue-in-cheek comment like that. I can only assume that he's maybe read too many books on spirituality, rather than trusting his gut feelings – certainly about past lives.

If you're bad – say, for example like my mother and father – I do not believe that you go to a good place when you pass. And I do not believe that you come back in spirit form in another body. When your physical body dies, I do not believe that you are given a chance to come back to be punished. I believe that you are denied any return. There's no way back for you. In my line of work, I've spoken to murderers, I've spoken to paedophile priests. I do know that there's no way back. Believe me: I know what I'm talking about.

I don't think somebody like William Roache is qualified to make a comment like that. Maybe he feels that his words were taken out of context. If they weren't, why would he even think along those lines? It does make me wonder how his mind works. Why is his thought pattern, his belief system, like that?

At the very least, I expected to receive an apology from him when he realised what he'd done. Not just for me but for everybody else he'd upset. I was mortified. Really, really mortified. But when I contacted the *Daily Star* and demanded a public apology from him, or even a meeting to tell him about my own experience and explain how hurtful his outburst had been, I heard nothing back.

He could do with spending an hour or two with me: I'm sure he'd have a different opinion after that. I don't believe for a minute that when people – murderers, rapists, paedophiles – behave the way they do in this life, that they are given another chance to come back and be punished. It just doesn't work like that. Some of us are given a chance if we want to come back, but I do believe that people who have done such horrendous things just disintegrate into the atmosphere and that's it. They're gone. That's why you get lost souls. I don't think that my dad will be coming back. Definitely, definitely not. I don't think that my mother will either.

I was so hurt and angry, I just wanted the chance to challenge him. I firmly believe that when you're quoted with a comment like that you should allow yourself to be challenged.

For the record, I do still watch *Coronation Street*. It's a traditional northern thing, something I've done for years. And I don't see him as anything but an actor out there doing his job, and doing it brilliantly. Good on him. I don't hate him or resent him, but I was disgusted by what he is alleged to have come out with.

Like I said, I believe in freedom of speech and all that, but his reported opinions were quite crushing, especially coming from a man who you can tell is highly intelligent and spiritual.

I like to think that I was speaking up for all abuse victims when I challenged him in the press. For those victims out there who might not be spiritual and who might have been left thinking, *Oh my god. What have I done to deserve this?* the answer is nothing. Nothing at all.

12

LITTLE JACK

Standing together at our bedroom window, Jack and I watched proudly as our strapping 16-year-old son, Jack Anthony, walked down the drive chatting away to his old pal James.

"He's so lovely, isn't he, our Jack?" I said to his dad. "He's growing up now, isn't he, Paula?" Jack replied. About five feet 10 inches tall, with his signature dark brown quiff of hair, dressed in the black skinny jeans and black jacket he'd agonised over earlier that day, 'Little' Jack (who'd started to moan about his nickname once he'd realised he was taller than his dad) looked absolutely gorgeous that day. We could both see that he was on the verge of manhood as he turned the corner of the hedge and disappeared out of sight. If only we'd known what lay ahead for him when he left us on that morning, Friday 2nd September 2016…

I think I struggled with his maturity more than his dad. It hadn't seemed so long ago that he'd come into my bedroom and sat on my bed, and I'd noticed something about him for the first time.

"Jack, lift your arm up," I'd instructed him, and he'd done as he was told. "Oh my god, Jack, you've got hairy armpits! You're not a little boy an more," I'd exclaimed, half embarrassing him and half making him laugh. He was growing into a big geezer and I didn't like it! The idea of him becoming a man had genuinely upset me. The youngest of my eight children, he was my baby and I'd always been over-protective of him. I'd smothered him since the day he was born, even though I'd never worried I'd lose him like I had Ashley. Even when, a couple of years earlier, I'd woken up very suddenly in the middle of the night with a distinctive voice in my head telling me, *Jack is going to go before you,* I hadn't thought for a split second that it was talking about my son, Little Jack.

Sitting bolt upright, I woke my husband, who was lying beside me, to tell him, "You're going to go before me, Jack." Later on I told my children as well.

"Please don't take Jack," I begged the Star People frantically. That same day, I can even remember telling Ashley, "You're safe. You're not going to die. It's lifted now; it's not you. I will now keep the two sons who are still here: Martin and Ashley." I had never felt for a minute that I would lose Martin, though – just Ash.

Nevertheless, any loving mother of any teenager worries about their son or daughter, and I was no exception in fretting about Jack at 16. It's normal.

Often he'd protest, "Oh Mum, stop worrying about me!" Or he'd say impatiently, "I'm OK, Mum!"

And he was, he really was. He was a good kid who didn't drink, take drugs or get into trouble with the police. Although he was shy, he'd fight back when we had a bit of banter about his newly sprouting moustache. His ambition was to go to university in Newcastle to study cyber security. He was an absolute whizz on a computer and he had a brilliant future ahead of him. No doubt about it. He was one cool geek! For the past three years he'd been helping me to run my Lillyanne Psychic Medium Facebook page. Ashley had set me up in my own online business towards the end of October 2013, so that I could give readings to people all around the world. For a couple of years before that, I'd been working for another psychic service as a telephone reader, having taken out an advertisement offering one-to-one readings in the local paper, *The Selby Times*. Like everybody else, I needed to earn a living – and still do – but it has always been a vocation for me rather than just a job. It's all part of 'The Deal' I made with my Star People in my mid-teens, allowing them to work with me and use me as a channel to pass messages on.

Now in my late 40s, it was the first time I'd used my psychic medium abilities to earn a proper living, and I'd chosen the name Lillyanne as my professional name because it was the name of my great-grandma on my mum's side of the family. Within no time, my reputation at the telephone reading service had grown and my popularity had escalated. Everybody wanted readings with me, and I was always fully booked. The scale of my success wasn't lost on Ashley, who told me one night that I was brilliant at what I did and that he was going to set me up with my own Facebook page so that I could work for myself.

"You'll never look back, Mum," he promised – and sure enough, within an hour of it going live for the first time, 300 people had clicked to 'like' my new interactive page.

Jack quickly became a dab hand at fixing any technical problems I had with my laptop, and I soon grew to rely on him. Whatever went wrong, he could always fix it within minutes, even when I got hacked. He'd try to explain to me what I needed to do but he'd laugh in disbelief and exasperation when I couldn't do what he could do so easily.

"Mum, why don't you understand it?" he'd ask me time after time, and I'd just shrug helplessly. Unlike his generation, mine hadn't been brought up with computers and it didn't come naturally.

Just before he'd gone out that September morning, Jack had been on his laptop, as usual. When he'd finished whatever he was doing, he'd come over, thrown his arms round me and said, "I love you, Mum," before giving me a big kiss and stroking my head. I just bombarded him with all the mum stuff after that. You know how you do!

"I'll be in about five for my tea," he added.

"Oh right, Jack. If you need me, call me."

"I know, Mum, I know."

"I love you, Bud. Enjoy your day," his dad told him, smiling proudly. I smiled with him, but I couldn't help thinking that

Jack looked a bit grey…

I'd wanted to drop him off in the car, but James had called and the plan was for them to walk into the village of Sherburn-in Elmet and get the bus to Selby, a journey of about half an hour. It was quite a big day out for Jack: he'd become quite reclusive over the past year, choosing to stay in all the time poring over his laptop. Even though we knew that a lot of teenagers did the same thing, his dad and I had worried a fair bit about that. We really wanted the day to be a happy and successful one for him.

I'd transferred £20 into his bank account so that he could get a burger or something to eat for his lunch. I've still got the change – about £7.50 or £7.80 – in his memory box, with a couple of receipts. The £5 note is an old one now, and the receipts have faded, but I'll never part with them. It's funny, the silly things you save. It's mad.

About half an hour after setting off, Jack had messaged me to go into his bedroom and get his PIN number. I'd done as he asked, and had rung him back rather than texting.

"Love you, Jack," I'd told him, as I usually did. Little did I realise – even with all my trusted psychic connections – that those would be the last words I would ever speak to him while he was alive.

I was on the phone to Ashley talking about work stuff when there came a knock at the door. It was Daisy, a local girl Little Jack knew, who told me, "You need to get down to Selby as fast as you can. They're trying to resuscitate Jack…"

"Ashley, I've got to put the phone down," I said, as Jack

and Katy ran down from upstairs.

In that very moment, I knew without a shadow of a doubt that he'd passed. I knew he was gone. Yet in my head I was still screaming, *No, no, no! Please don't take Jack.*

Katy tried to reassure me by saying, "Mum, calm down. He'll be having a panic attack." But I knew differently.

"He's not coming home," I told his dad as we all got into the car, him in the front passenger seat, me in the driving seat and Katy in the back.

As a psychic medium, you really can't read yourself. It's impossible. And if ever I've proved that point, it was the night I misinterpreted that voice in my head: *Jack is going to go before you.* I'd got it wrong. It was my son Jack who would go before me, not my husband Jack. It was only later, when my husband Jack pointed out that until recent years he had always been known as Jackie rather than Jack, that this clicked.

By this time, Ashley had managed to get hold of someone who told him that Little Jack had suffered a complete respiratory collapse and was en-route in an ambulance to a hospital in York. Driving along, I kept saying to my Star People, "You've taken Little Jack, haven't you? Rather than Ashley." Suddenly, it all made sense: the warning I'd had from them after John had died. Little Jack was the *one more to go.*

At the traffic lights at Selby, I did a sudden U-turn and headed for home.

"My son is already gone. I know he's already gone," I repeated to Jack and Katy.

"He's not there." I was referring to the hospital he'd been taken to. I knew his spirit was whooshing around, that he was not coming back to us. Although I didn't hear his voice, I had a very strong feeling that he was telling me, "Go home, Mum, and make yourself a sweet cup of tea."

Stopping to let Jack and Katy out of the car to make their own way to the hospital, I headed home alone to a cup of PG Tips and eight or nine Kalms herbal tablets for stress and anxiety. Afterwards I climbed into Jack's bed, where I rocked. I tidied the house and then screamed hysterically to Archangel Michael, demanding to know, "Why have you taken my son? Why have you done this?" I didn't get any response.

Phoning Joanne in Leeds, I told her my gut feeling, that Little Jack had died – and immediately afterwards, I received a call from a nurse at the hospital.

"Mrs Bairstow, you need to get here," she advised. "Your son is gravely ill."

But I knew he had already gone. I would not have been fit to drive anyway. I was hysterical, as you can imagine, and the multiple Kalms tablets I'd taken would not have helped. No way would I have been as brave as Jack and Katy, who had gone to the hospital to see Jack one last time. It just wouldn't have been doable for me. So I told her I would not be able to make it, that I knew he'd already gone and that I did not need to see him laid out in a hospital bed. She said that she just needed to inform me that if I wanted to get there, to get there now.

Funnily enough, Ashley – who, like Demi, has inherited some of my psychic abilities – knew as well. While driving to the hospital with his partner Kyle, he suddenly heard his brother's voice in his left ear informing him, "I'm over here, Ashley, but I'm all right."

My own gut feeling, along with Ashley's premonition, was confirmed soon afterwards by Katy, who phoned from the hospital screaming hysterically, "He's died. We've lost our Little Jack, Mum."

Afterwards, a lovely senior registrar phoned from the hospital to say she was so, so sorry and to let me know that they'd done the very best in their power for my son, but that he had passed away. Two whole hours they'd tried, the traumatised staff, to resuscitate him. I can remember her telling me that, altogether, there had been 15 people there trying to bring him back to life. God bless that hospital in York. They really did go the extra mile that day for Jack. They did a fantastic job and I really would love to have thanked them all personally. The registrar seemed close to tears herself. I think she was trying to hold them back for me. She said, "Actually, I am going to be honest with you: this has traumatised two of my staff so much that they are going to need counselling." I'll never forget her words. She said, "It's not every day we see this." She might well have had a couple of kids herself. Who knows? Whether she had kids or not, hers wasn't an easy job to do that day.

As we began to fit the pieces of the tragic jigsaw together, we discovered that Jack had collapsed outside the hardware store Wilko in the centre of Selby. After getting off the bus, he and James had pottered about for a bit. Jack had withdrawn the £20 I'd transferred into his account and bought his last lunch – two battered sausages with curry sauce – when he'd developed a tickly cough. Heading to Sainsbury's to buy a cold drink of Lucozade, he hadn't felt any better and had told James he needed to get the next bus home. Although it was only a very short walk from Wilco to the bus stop, he couldn't walk and needed to hold on to the walls. After telling James to call for an ambulance, he sat down on a bench and seemed to calm down, before starting to turn purple from the neck up and falling to the floor. James and passers-by did what they could to help as ambulance staff tried to shout instructions down James' phone, but it was no good. God bless the staff in Wilko and Sainsbury's, who covered him with blankets and brought out chairs to screen the area when the two ambulances turned up. Refusing to give in, the ambulance staff kept going, going, going, but only ever managed to get a slight heartbeat back. He asphyxiated, and never came back.

I can remember lots of people arriving at the house, including Ashley. I will never forget the frozen expression on his face. Emotionless. He literally fell into my arms and so did his partner Kyle, who was with him. I can remember hugging them both and saying, "Look, it's OK. Calm down. We will sort this out. We will get through this. We have got to be strong now for Jack. We all need each other now more than ever." I said the same thing to Katy and to Jack, his dad, when they arrived a bit later. It was just pandemonium, as you can probably imagine, and I was starting to feel confused, as if there had been a mistake. I went into shock mode, but at 5am the following morning, it hit me. My body was freezing cold despite my pyjamas and woolly socks, and I started shaking from head to foot.

"You've got to go on," was all my Star People would tell me at that point. "You can't go under. We told you that you had to be strong."

The worst part for Jack, my husband, was having to officially identify his only son, who looked absolutely perfect. Apparently he still had a slight flush in his cheeks.

"Why, Jack? Why, why?" he kept asking him, unable to leave his side. He felt completely demolished, completely dumbfounded. We all did. Ashley couldn't stop being sick. It was heart-breaking. Afterwards, Jack and I both sat at the top of the garden, needing to be out of the way, alone in our grief.

My belief is that the body is a beautiful vessel that houses the spirit. Once I knew his spirit was no longer there, I did not want to see the empty vessel and refused to see him at the chapel of rest. That's how I dealt with it. And I didn't want everybody else gawping over him there, either. Little Jack was a very private person and I know he'd have hated it. In the end only five people – four of whom were exceptionally close to him – visited him there.

I told Jack that I felt it was his place to choose Little Jack's clothes, and he picked out a pair of his black skinny jeans, a burgundy t-shirt, his black jacket, yellow socks and a pair of his own Calvin Klein boxer shorts. Katy put a Buddha bracelet on Jack's wrist and, on my behalf, sprinkled frankincense at his head, hands and feet. It is an old ritual to protect the spirit from negative energies. I knew Little Jack's spirit had already gone to the light, but I just wanted him to smell gorgeous. On his chest, she placed a photo of me and a piece of my hair. I wanted to make sure a part of me went with him. I also felt very strongly that Jack shouldn't have a traditional funeral with a black hearse and heavy wooden coffin, so we instructed our local funeral directors, Thorntons, that we wanted a wicker coffin and a white Mercedes Benz to carry him on his final journey. They arranged it all perfectly.

Strangely, 10 days before he passed, I'd wandered into our local St Mary's Parish Church with Jack for the first time. It's a beautiful ancient stone church with architecture that dates back to the period 1225-1250. You can smell the oldness of it! We'd been wandering round the grounds and, seeing that it was open, had popped our heads round the door to ask a cleaner in there if we could go in to take a few photographs. Well, I've always felt that I was surrounded by angels but never more so than when I saw the pictures Jack took of me in there, which showed a blue aura all around me. I felt that somehow we'd been meant to visit the church when we did, and it seemed more than fitting that the remembrance service for Jack should be at St Mary's. The vicar, John, was absolutely brilliant in his service. Jack and some of Little Jack's siblings and friends lit candles for him as part of the service, and Ashley gave a wonderful eulogy. Demi chose 'Somewhere Over the Rainbow' for a happy, uplifting song. I chose 'Green Eyes' by Coldplay because he'd once told me that that was my song: he was always fascinated by how my own eyes changed colour – from blue-green to almost purple with a yellow ring round my pupils. Everybody was asked not to wear black, so nobody did. We wanted it to be a celebration of Little Jack's life and I can honestly say it was a real spiritual send off. If Little Jack had been able to choose his own funeral, I think he'd have chosen the same – right down to the fireworks we let off and the Chinese chicken curry (his favourite) that we served up back at the house afterwards.

Earlier the same day, at 10am, a small service was held at Lawnswood Crematorium in Leeds. I was adamant that I wasn't going to that, because I had a very strong feeling that I shouldn't. "Don't go there. If you go, you'll drop," my Star People had warned.

And I knew they were right. I would have keeled over. Attending one funeral service there, with a son in a little white coffin, had been bad enough.

I'd struggled with the arrangements throughout: I didn't seem to know what I wanted. None of it, of course, but that was out of my hands and practical choices had to be made. At first I'd wanted to bring Little Jack home with a traditional wake the night before the funeral, so that I could sit up all night with him lying in his coffin in the living room. But Katy, who was brilliant at organising everything for me, persuaded me against that.

"Have you any idea what it's going to do to you when they put the lid on in the morning?" she asked. "You will not want to let him go."

She was right, of course. Something in me clicked and I changed my mind completely. I didn't even want to see Jack's coffin. Nor did I want the hearse to pull onto the drive on the baking hot day of the funeral, 13th September 2016. I even went around the house and closed all the blinds so that I wouldn't see it through the windows. My brother Anthony stayed with me and made me a cup of tea.

"Don't let anyone come in to see me, and don't let me see the hearse," I urged him. "I don't want to see it."

People did try to come in to see me, but he wouldn't let them into the living room. He was a tower of strength, our Anthony.

"You don't have to go out there if you don't want to," he reassured me.

When the hearse arrived at the end of the drive, Katy came in and told me, "He's here now, Mum, on the drive."

"Katy, I don't want to see it. Please ask them to take him off the drive and straight to Lawnswood. Tell them to take him now," I told her.

"OK, Mum, it's your call," she replied. "Sit down and drink your cup of tea with Anthony."

She'd only been gone maybe a minute, though, when I changed my mind again and announced to Anthony, "I've got to go out there. I'm his mum. It's bad enough me not going to Lawnswood. I've got to go and touch his casket and kiss it." I fled out of the door.

The back of the white hearse was already up, and I could see the shape of my beloved Little Jack lying in the wicker coffin. I'll never forget it. Everything went deathly quiet as, propped up by my brother Anthony and one of my children's aunties, I lay my hands on top of the coffin.

"It's OK, Jack. I'm not going to keep you here for long. I know you couldn't stand the sun," I joked with him for the very last time. Knowing that he wouldn't want everybody standing around staring, I kissed the coffin, which was topped with a big wreath of lovely white and purple flowers, and told the funeral directors to take him on his journey. Bless them, they even wore purple handkerchiefs in their top pockets because it was Little Jack's favourite colour. Beside the coffin the word SON was spelt out in huge red rose letters.

With that, I went back inside the house, where my brother Anthony stayed with me.

I was told afterwards that, as the hearse passed Sherburn High School, where Jack had been a pupil, his whole year group was standing outside to pay their respects. On the drive to Lawnswood, the Queen song 'You're My Best Friend' was played in the car because that was the song I'd once dedicated to Jack after he'd calmed me down when I was anxious.

"You know you've got healing abilities, Jack. Not many people can calm me down," I'd told him. And it was true. He was my best friend.

The official post mortem report cited the cause of Little Jack's death as a chronic bronchial asthma attack. It's true that he was a known asthmatic and that he was under the care of the family doctor for various allergies. He'd first been given an inhaler when he was about 10 or 11 and a pupil at Athelstan Community Primary School. I'd got one too as we both had tickly coughs. I still get mine. Allergies to trees, pollen and rapeseed were blamed and Jack was examined goodness knows how many times for quite a few years. One time he was having what looked to me like a panic attack and, just to be on the safe side, I took him to the surgery to be checked out. Thankfully I was given an emergency appointment and he was seen by a locum doctor from London. He looked at his notes and picked up on the fact that I'd been taking Jack to the doctor for a while with similar symptoms – eyes watering, nose running and tickly cough. After examining him, he diagnosed asthma and went on to explain that allergies and asthma were closely linked. That really rocked me. I'd seen him go a bit panicky sometimes, like me, but I'd never seen him have anything like an asthma attack. I think it was at that point that he was prescribed a brown preventative inhaler. A couple of times he'd gone to hospital in York to get his oxygen levels back up. The last time had been was just three weeks before he passed: that night, he'd felt that his chest was tight and that he couldn't catch his breath.

"I haven't got an inhaler, Mum. You're going to have to call an ambulance, because asthma can kill you," he'd told me.

Although he didn't use his inhaler much in front of me, he seemed to use it constantly when I wasn't around. Over a 10-month period, he'd been prescribed with 42 inhalers. Obviously an excessive amount. But other than that, he was as fit as hell. He and his dad could walk and chat, father to son, for miles and miles.

So that night, as any good mother would, I did as he asked and called an ambulance out to him. The paramedics tested his oxygen saturation levels and said that everything was fine – but as a precaution, due to his medical history, they took him to hospital. Because of my agoraphobia I couldn't go with him, but Jack went. When they arrived, his oxygen saturation levels had plummeted and it took three to four hours to get them back to normal. He was allowed out again in the early hours with a blue inhaler and 20 steroid tablets. He was also given a warning from a doctor that he must use his preventer inhaler and reduce the amount of times he was using his reliever one. And that was it. He felt fine when he got back home.

Despite all this, I still choose to believe to this day that it was a cardiac arrest, not asthma, that took Jack – and with good reason.

Within a week of his passing, Little Jack came to me while I was laying on my bed. I wasn't asleep, so it wasn't a dream.

"Mum," called a familiar voice.

"Jack?" I yelled.

"Mum, I'm here. Please, Mum, please don't worry about me. I am OK."

Seizing my opportunity, I asked, "What happened on that day?"

"It wasn't an asthma attack,' he replied.

"Who came for you?" I wanted to know.

"Our John, and he's here for you."

I always have to question everything, so I asked, "How did you recognise John?"

"By his eyes," he told me matter-of-factly.

I knew then that he wasn't mistaken. John had really big, steely blue eyes, light rather than dark.

"Auntie Janet's here as well," he went on. Sadly my old friend, Jack's lovely sister, who had brought us together, had also passed before Jack.

"There are so many people here telling me they're family. What a fabulous place this is!"

It was a relief that he thought so, because a couple of weeks before he passed he'd asked me to tell him what Heaven looked like. Ever since I was a little girl, I'd seen occasional glimpses of Heaven and I tried to explain to him about the more vibrant colours you see up there: the bluer skies, the multi-coloured birds and different plants and trees. All in a bright, light, healing setting. Looking back, it's so uncanny that he should question me like that when he did. He'd never asked me anything like it before. Equally uncanny is the number of birds that seemed to appear all around the house in the last couple of weeks of his life, all singing merrily. There was one beady eyed robin that turned up all the time, constantly on watch for us. Looking back, I believe it was a message from the spirits telling me to get ready or prepare for something. I strongly believe that. I actually even put the video up on my Facebook page, telling people that this little robin had been coming and tweeting every day. "I wonder what message he has for me, folks," I said. Little Jack died about four months later.

Still sounding happy, Little Jack asked me to go into his old bedroom, which hasn't been changed since the day he left it. I did as he asked, and when I was in his old bed, he told me that the beige colour of the walls was the same colour as those in the chapel of rest and described the layout of the room where his body had spent its final hours. Less than 24 hours. He also told me how Katy had been brushing his hair to get his quiff the way he liked it as he lay in his coffin. All of a sudden, she'd dropped the hair brush on his shoulder and panicked.

"Please mention that to Katy, Mum," he said, chuckling at the memory. Then *bang!* As fast as he'd come into the room, he was gone.

When I quizzed Katy about the colour and layout of chapel of rest and the dropped hairbrush, she confirmed everything. If there'd been any doubt whatsoever that it was Jack who had come to me, it vanished into thin air.

Like John, Little Jack helps me with my work. He guides me

all the time. I am sure that his spiritual essence is here every single day, and when I do readings I can feel him around. I still feel he's part of my Facebook page.

After this visit, I started to dream about him.

"You know who it is, Mum," he'd tell me.

At that point, I knew that my spiritual journey was really going to take off.

Whitkirk Church, Leeds

My son Little Jack

My son Little Jack

My son Little Jack

My sons Ashley and Little Jack

My son Little Jack

My sons Ashley and Little Jack

13

THE BOND THAT CAN'T BE BROKEN

Demi

I can still vividly remember the day my mum and my stepdad, Big Jack, came home from hospital with Little Jack.

He was all wrapped up in a blue shawl in Mum's arms when I saw him for the first time, and I just felt absolutely amazed by this small baby. It was instant love. I was only four years old myself, and as the youngest child in my family I'd never had a younger sibling before, so I wasn't used to being around babies. I was still a baby myself really. But I just loved him.

I remember he used to cry a lot in the early days, though, and Mum would freak out because sometimes he'd go a funny colour and faint. She took him to the doctor, who said it was normal and that he'd grow out of it – and sure enough, he did. He was a cool little guy and I was besotted.

I used to try and feed him, and I once accidentally got milk in his eye. He was still only tiny – maybe a few months old – and I thought that I'd blinded him. I cried for ages thinking that I'd hurt him. My mum had to really reassure me that I hadn't! It's funny because even though I was only young myself I felt a real duty of care towards him. I suppose that's what being a big sister is. And I loved being a big sister. I was so proud. I'd love to be able to say that I had an older sibling back then to look up to myself, but by that time we'd moved away from Leeds and they weren't around so much. It was just me and Little Jack. That's probably why we were so close: we grew up together, it was always the two of us. When he was a toddler we moved back to Leeds; he started going to the nursery at my primary school and I'd always walk him in, holding his hand. He used to love that, and would beam up at me. I think I was in Year Three when we first walked in together, but it carried on for years!

It was quite a turbulent childhood for us because of some of the things that were going off in the family, but ultimately it was a happy one for us. Really happy. Little Jack was my main person, the only friend I had at home apart from my parents. I suppose he was my first ever friend who wasn't my mum or dad.

We would always play together, usually on the Game Boy. Though it was officially his, he shared with me. He absolutely loved Pokemon, and we'd sit for hours playing it together. There was a Harry Potter game we really liked playing as well.

That's not to say the sharing didn't cause a few arguments, of course! I remember that, one day, he got into a mood when he wanted to do something and couldn't, and he threw it in my direction and it broke in half. Yet my mum blamed it on me! She said, "Demi, what on Earth did you do that for?" The cheek! Luckily she fell soft, though, and bought us another one.

We used to watch videos together a lot as well – Disney films mostly. My favourite was *The Lion King* and Jack's was *The Jungle Book*. The songs in it used to really make him laugh. His favourite was 'I Wanna be Like You', with King Louie's 'Oh obee do' chorus, which Jack loved. He used to sing that quite a bit.

We've got a family tradition of opening one present each on Christmas Eve and obviously, being kids, we always chose the biggest ones we could see. One Christmas Eve when I was about 10 and Jack was four or five and we were living in a hostel in Tadcaster, I opened my parcel to find a big white teddy. I've still got it upstairs. Jack opened his to find a Baloo bear. We were both really, really pleased that year. Jack absolutely loved Baloo. When he wasn't carrying him around with him, he sat him on his bed. Baloo is still upstairs as well. Mum's explained since that they were donated from somewhere and given to her to wrap up for us by the hostel warden-cum-social worker. Despite the circumstances, I've still got loads of happy memories of my childhood spent with Jack.

We went through a phase of pretending to be spies, and would spy on my mum and dad when they were doing completely normal things like just washing up! We'd leap all over the place pretending that we were on secret missions. Mum and Dad would go along with it as well. The age gap between Jack and me was never an issue, I think because we went from home to home together so much. We were always a constant in each other's lives. If we'd lived in one place forever I think we would probably have had our own separate friends, instead of just being with each other.

When I was about 12 and Jack was seven or eight, we were watching out of his bedroom window here in Sherburn-in-Elmet and we saw a round thing in the sky. We watched it for ages because even at that age, Jack had a fascination with the planets. It was a green-y colour and it was going back and forth making a choking noise, and then suddenly it burst into white light. It sounds absolutely crazy, I know, but we both saw it. To this day I still don't have a clue what it was. Maybe a spaceship? It was definitely something strange. I can't think of anything else that would do that. When we told my mum, she said, "Are you sure it wasn't a firework?" But we were both adamant that is wasn't, and told her a bit indignantly, "Yes we're sure!" To be honest, we were both scared.

As he grew into his teens, Little Jack became quite a private person. But I always said to him that if he needed to talk to me, he could – that I'd always be there for him. Just as I had been when he was being bullied at school a few years before. When he was about seven and I was about 12, this horrible boy was kicking him, calling him names and making his life quite miserable really at playtimes. He was awful to everybody in general, but when he started targeting my little brother, I thought, *I'm not having this.* It went on for a couple of weeks and I was absolutely seething about it. One day I'd had enough. I knew he was in a nearby park, so I went up and smacked him across the face and warned him, "If you ever go near him again, I'll bray you!" I'm not normally a violent person at all; I think the reason I was so angry was because he wasn't Jack's age, he was my age. I thought, *Well Jack can't stick up for himself against somebody so much bigger and older than him, so I will!* I was fiercely protective of my little brother and I thought, *I'm not having that!* The bullying soon fizzled out after I'd confronted him. He left Jack alone after that. I think Mum was quite proud of me!

I think that being around my biological dad a lot and coming from a traumatised home affected me, even though I never saw anything out of the ordinary going on. I think I must have just sensed that things weren't quite right. When Mum and my stepdad Jack first got together, I was only three and I was quite scared of guys in general, so I was scared of him. Even though he was really nice to me, I wouldn't go near him and I used to hide behind wardrobes and cupboards and stuff. I also had nightmares growing up, which lasted until I was about 12, so I would often get up in the middle of the night and crawl into Little Jack's bed and sleep with him. For some reason, even though he was only a little kid, he made me feel safe. He was always there and it was just really nice.

We didn't really argue much – though I'm not going to lie and say we never rowed! We had fights. Physical fights! I think we both thought we were Rocky Balboa! I think my stepdad got us both into those films. We'd start out by playfighting, but it would often end up in a big, proper fight, with one of us hurting the other. We always made up pretty quickly though! It never lasted for long. We'd fight and then we'd be OK straight after. I remember once I bit him; another time when I was about eight, he whacked me on the nose with a really heavy hair brush. Mum blamed me again and then everybody at school started calling me Rainbow Nose because I had a big raised lump on my nose.

One of my fondest memories has to be from the time we spent in a Catholic school. We were both in the same nativity play: I was an angel and he was a shepherd. We didn't have the greatest costumes – I think they were made from old sheets – and we had to sing a song called 'Fishing for Stars' in this dusty old hall. That was a really precious time, that. So many happy memories.

I can remember watching *The Simpsons* and *SpongeBob SquarePants* together. He loved *The Simpsons* and thought *SpongeBob* was so funny. *The Cramp Twins* and *Courage the Cowardly Dog* were other favourites. We used to watch them all on the Sky TV Kids channel when we came in from school. We used to read as well: I read him my *Horrible Histories* books. Some of them had songs in them, so I'd sing them to him. I remember once there was a song about a kid who died.

I sang it to my little brother and he started crying. I said, "I'm so sorry!" He was really soft-hearted, bless him. At Christmas we used to watch *The Snowman* together, and he absolutely loved it until it got to the part where 'Walking in the Air' came on and he knew the snowman was about to melt; he'd start crying before it even happened. Thinking about it, a lot of my happy memories with Jack are centred round Christmas. It was always such a special time in our house. Now we all just collectively get through the day: we always get to a point where we just sit and stare at each other, because we don't know how to feel or what to do.

I feel Jack's loss most at the end of the year. As soon as the seasons start to change, I know it's going to be a weird few months for me. Because of my mum's agoraphobia we didn't really go on summer holidays, which was fine because we were happy anyway. We'd run all over the place. When I was very little and thin, we would climb under the school fence and go and run around the school field together. But my happiest memories with Jack are from autumn and wintertime, from Halloween onwards. I remember my dad once bought him a blue vampire mask from the supermarket for Halloween. Bonfire nights were big occasions too: we'd have a bonfire in the garden, wherever we were, and I've got so many funny memories from bonfire nights. My dad nailed a Catherine wheel to the fence one year, but it came off and went whizzing round the garden! Ask my mum – he's not great at DIY! Since we've lived here, we've always been able to see the big community bonfire perfectly from the end of our drive. People used to travel from miles around to see it, but we didn't even need to leave home. We loved fireworks. Every New Year's Eve – before I turned 13 and started going to my friends' houses to celebrate – we'd sit and watch Big Ben chiming at midnight together on TV. Mum always insisted! They're very precious memories now. I feel sad, but at the same time it's a bittersweet thing remembering times that are so precious.

I'd moved out of home less than a year before Jack passed away, and I don't think my brain adjusted to coming back to this house without him here for a long time. My mum would say, "I'll shout Jack," and I'd ask, "Big or Little Jack?" when there was only one to shout… Then it would all just come back to me and I would think, *Oh God, I can't believe you've gone.*

Even now, I'll come to the house with my partner Darren and just for a fleeting moment I'll think that Little Jack will be upstairs. But of course he isn't. Sometimes I see stuff – gadgets and funny things – in shops that I know he'd like, and I'll think about buying it for him, even though I know he's not here. Once, six months after he passed, I was even thinking of getting him some tickets to see Drake, the Canadian rapper he liked. I just saw them advertised when I was online and thought, *Jack would like that.* Then I remembered that he's not here anymore. I still do things like that now.

Before Jack's passing, I really felt as if I had my life in order. I was living in a flat in Selby with my friend and working in town, at the local Costa cafe. After leaving school at 16, I'd gone to college for three years to do a BTEC qualification in Travel and Tourism. I'm good at academic stuff when I want to be. Like my mum, I'm good at English and History – but I like learning on my own terms, not someone else's. When I'm well enough, I might do an Open University degree course in English or something so that I can take everything at my own pace. I'd like to work with people in the future – maybe counselling. Poor Jack doesn't have a future and I'm so sad about what could have been. He was so clever, really technically minded. It was quite something to see it, sometimes. A proper whizz! I remember watching him coding when he was about 13, and asking him, "How on Earth do you do that?" He just told me to stop disturbing him because he was concentrating! He used to help Mum out with her business, too. He would have been at university by now and I would have been so proud to see him graduate.

My mum says that Jack was gutted when I moved out, but he was old enough to realise we were growing up. We probably took each other for granted a bit when we were living together, but afterwards we seemed to grow closer again. He would always message me on Facebook and ask me how I was. We had so many plans. He was going to come over and stay with me when he started Selby College but, of course, he died before he started. I was going to take him to York for the day.

I often think about all the big moments in our lives that he's going to miss, like my wedding day. He won't meet Joanne's child, our Devantae Jack, who was born in August 2017, almost a year after his namesake passed. If I have kids, he won't meet any of them. It just makes me really sad. However, I am going to make sure that any kids I have always know about him, their Uncle Jack, even though he's not here. He will definitely live on in us. It comes back to Christmas time again: I think about being 35, with maybe a couple of kids in tow, going round doing all the Christmas family visiting. He's someone we should be going to see, and that makes me really sad.

I sometimes think about the point in the future when so much time will have passed that he will have been gone longer than the 16 years and eight months he was with us. It's going to be really strange when that time comes. I'm not looking forward to it. It affects you for the rest of your life. You learn to live with it but I don't think that grief will ever fully heal for me. I'd like to say that I have learned to live with it, but sometimes when it hits me that he's not here, it gives me a panic attack. The only thing that would make it go away is to see him again, and I can't. It's really bad when that happens because it's so overwhelming. Sometimes when it happens I go and sit in his bedroom because I feel a bit closer to him there. If I'm staying here, I often sleep downstairs on the floor at first, or on the sofa, to be near his ashes. In the early days, Mum would often come down in the morning and catch me asleep there because I'd been restless in the night and unable to sleep upstairs. Being downstairs near his ashes was the only thing that made me feel better.

Some of my nicest memories up to the age of 12 are of time spent with my mum's mum, my Nanna Pauline. Those memories have since been stained because of what I now know about her. Before I found all that out, though, she was the perfect nan to me. She'd have me to stay at her house every weekend and take me out shopping to buy toys and clothes and books – just anything I wanted really. We'd eat ice cream together and it was just really, really nice. But she never asked Jack to go over with me. I said to her a few times, "Can we get Jack something?" I'd even try and sneak stuff into her shopping basket: little toy cars and action figures. She'd buy me all this stuff and I'd feel really bad taking it home. It was as if I was rubbing his face in it. I felt like he was getting left out. She just never make a fuss of him. It was like I was the only one who existed. I'd come home quite upset about it sometimes.

Nanna Pauline was dead to me as soon as I was old enough to realise the severity of what went on. I just stopped talking to her and never really acknowledged her again. I just realised that she was the not the person I thought she was. I was never actually told what had happened to my mum, but I heard things during family arguments. We were never really shielded from it. And then there was the court case. I was 15 when all that was going on. It was a confusing time, and quite jarring to think that that lovely old lady had turned out to be quite evil.

She treated Jack quite differently. She just never really acknowledged him. You can even see it in all the old family photos: there are so many of me being taken to see Santa and having little parties at her house, but Jack isn't in any of them. He was never, ever invited. On birthdays I'd get loads of money from family, but I don't remember them ever doing that for Little Jack. On some occasions, I'd give him half my money because I felt so bad. I was only young, but I knew something wasn't right about the way he was being treated. Although he never said anything to me, he would look a bit sad sometimes and you could tell it got to him.

He grew up disliking our Nanna Pauline. It was like she was punishing him for being Big Jack's son and not my biological father's son, who she really had up on a pedestal. She really romanticised who he was, and she never liked Big Jack. It was as if she begrudged Mum moving on. I've only come to realise that as I've got older and been able to look at the situation with a more mature head on my shoulders. Beforehand, I loved Little Jack so much that I just couldn't understand why I was getting all this preferential treatment. My stepdad's mum, Alma, didn't behave like that. Little Jack was her biological grandson and I was no blood relation, but she didn't treat us any differently at Christmas time – or at any other time. She was always fair. The way my Nanna Pauline behaved just made me feel guilty and horrible, even though it wasn't my fault: I was just a kid in the middle.

There was one Christmas, when I was about 10 and Jack was six, when it just got embarrassing. She gave Jack one present – a £10 red plastic bus from Asda – and I got a whole pile worth about £150: Bratz dolls, make up sets, annuals. My mum says I threw them in the bin. As an adult now, I cannot imagine why you would ever treat people like that. It wasn't normal. Very strange. Everyone preferred me, but that's not a happy memory.

It's nicer to remember the good times. Like walking, hand in hand, to school together in our blue jumpers when we moved here. By the time he was seven or eight, he didn't want to hold my hand any more as he wanted to walk with his mates, and he'd run off. I used to insist on seeing him into his classroom though, even if it made me late going into mine. Even now if I look out of the upstairs bedroom windows, I can see us both walking across the field together to get to school. Sometimes we'd look back and Mum and Dad would be at the window waving goodbye to us. That's a really fond memory. Really happy.

When I was in my final year at high school and Jack was in his first, it was so funny: he'd get so embarrassed by me. He'd be with all his cool little friends, but I'd still go up and ask him how he was and how his day was going. I just wanted him to know that if he was having trouble settling in, I was there for him. He was fine, though, and he'd just tell me to go away! I think by then he was sick of me. He let go before I did!

On the night before we lost Jack, I'd spent the night here. He'd been texting me to see if I wanted some of the spaghetti Bolognese that Katy had made, but when I arrived it was quite late – about 11.30pm – and everybody was in bed, including Jack. I listened on the landing but just assumed they were all asleep, so I went to bed too. I didn't see him the next morning either, as I set off to work before he was up and left without saying goodbye. It's such a shame how that happened, because nine times out of 10 I would have gone into his room and sat on his bed and we'd have had a chat. What's worse is that I later discovered that he'd told Mum he'd been awake all night.

It was a completely normal day at work, making coffee for people, but then Ashley rang me sounding really scared. At first I didn't realise anything was wrong because I was in work mode, but he said to me, "Demi, you really need to come home now. You need to come back to Mum's." Not realising what had happened, I said, "I can't come home yet. I have to lock up. What do you want?" His voice broke and he said, "No Demi, you need to come home right now." And then I knew that something wasn't right. I grabbed my stuff and asked my supervisor if I could leave. Unbeknown to me, Ashley had already phoned and told her there'd been a bereavement. I was the last person to know because everybody was too scared to tell me. It was a really hot day and I was panicking, so I got a taxi and rang my mum. My sister Joanne answered her phone. I started screaming at her, wanting to know what was going on. At first I thought I'd lost my mum – but then she took the phone off Joanne and told me that Jack had died. At that, I had the worst panic attack I've ever had. I screamed at the taxi driver to let me out and I ran into the street. Outside Wetherspoons I just started shouting for help, but then I suddenly thought that maybe I'd just misheard Mum, and

I rang her back. She told me what had happened, but my brain just couldn't deal with it. The whole day is a blur. I was hysterical.

I phoned work and a colleague arrived to take me to Darren's house. He didn't really know what to say: we were both so shocked that we just stared at each other. I didn't know what to do so I just walked round his garden in circles. His mum took me home and there were loads of people there. I was like a zombie and my stepdad was crying, but my poor mum was just on autopilot. It affects people differently.

I've never felt pain like it in my life. It actually hurt: my heart hurt. I felt like I'd been stabbed in the chest or something.

The day of Jack's funeral was the day he was supposed to start college, and he was being cremated instead. Like my mum, I didn't go to the chapel of rest to see him or to the first part of his funeral. I just couldn't deal with anything to do with his body, and I'm happy I didn't. I think it would have pushed me over the edge.

I went to the church service after the cremation, where I sat between my mum and my stepdad. They both held my hands. 'Somewhere over the Rainbow' was played, like I'd asked. We'd always watched *The Wizard of Oz* together when we were little. I can't watch it now. I think of Dorothy saying, "There's no place like home!" and it just reminds me that this will never feel like home again.

The weeks and months afterwards are just a blur. I became severely depressed and couldn't go back to work. I just stayed in bed. I didn't have a bath for weeks and my hair – once my pride – became really matted. The panic attacks got much worse and I started to develop agoraphobia. Darren just had to carry me through it all. He was amazing, so understanding. He never judged me. After a few months he persuaded me to go on antidepressants. It was a really dark time.

I wouldn't answer phone calls from my family, and I couldn't go back inside our house for months. I stayed with my friend Leverett and her husband Andy in their spare room instead. They were so nice to me. Some of my friends sent me little care packages; everybody was so sweet and kind, especially my mum's friend Dawn, who was there for us all.

When I did go home again six or nine months later, I had to sit with my back to Jack's ashes. I could not look at them. But then one night things changed, and I asked Mum if I could have a look at them. She took the lid off and I kissed some and felt some sort of relief. More peaceful.

Losing Jack was a massive shock. I knew he had asthma, but I'd never seen him have an attack.

Time has helped a little. It's like we are just now starting to get our heads around it. The first year was just a blur. Soon after it happened, a complete stranger recognised my mum, approached her in the street and threw her arms round her. She explained that she'd lost a son too, and told her that although it had got easier, the scar would always be there. I think she was right.

Drawing by my daughter Demi

Top two photos: My son Little Jack and daughter Demi
Bottom photo: My son Little Jack, husband Jack and daughter Demi

14

SUCCESS AND SURVIVAL

Even though I can still feel Little Jack around me every day in so many spiritual ways – like I can still feel John – I do miss being able to give him a great big hug. What loving mother wouldn't?

It's an enormous comfort to me that a tiny physical part of him remains here, taking pride of place in the corner of our living room, the heart of our home. Some people like to scatter the ashes of loved ones; others like to bury them. I have never wanted to do either of those things, which is why the globe urn containing Little Jack's remains forms the centre of a family shrine, surrounded by candles, cards, poems, personal bits and bobs and photographs that change all the time. Hanging above it is a very special photograph that Ashley managed to commission from a company endorsed by the National Aeronautics and Space Administration (NASA), which shows the cosmic alignment of the stars above the hospital where he was born at the exact time of his birth. There are seven: one star for each sibling, including John, whom Little Jack will have met for the first time in the spirit world. Little Jack was always fascinated by space and full of wonder about the stars. You did your brother proud there, Ash.

As soon as I've finished working on this book, the first published copy will be laid in the shrine too. I hope I've done him equally proud. I know it's what Little Jack wanted because it was all his idea originally. As soon as my own star started to rise as my alter ego, Lillyanne Psychic Medium, he was every bit as excited as I was. "You'll be a household name one day, Mum," he proudly predicted. "Smash it! Write a book! Go for it!" So far, so good. Today, Lillyanne (with her backcombed hair and heavier make up than Paula Bairstow) is known across the world thanks to the wonders of social media, the technical abilities of Little Jack and the business nous of Ashley. Not forgetting my loyal Star People and my spirit friends, of course. Without them I would be nobody. With them, I have a database of nearly half a million fans, and I receive hundreds of messages containing amazing feedback every single day. Although my success has meant that I can't deal with every one personally and have had to employ a team of 70 carefully vetted psychic readers, I still like to give back as much as I can by going live on the Facebook page every day and giving away 400 free readings to people every month. I'm also reaching out to people with a new column in a national psychic magazine, and plans are afoot to go out and do a live psychic tour, anxiety permitting. It's massively important to me to give back, which is largely why I do what I do. I'd be lying if

I said the money isn't nice, of course. It's enabled me to have a stable life for the first time ever: a semi-detached family house and a nice Mercedes Benz car that I've bought myself. Last Christmas, a bittersweet time that I find extremely difficult to deal with without Little Jack, I even bought myself a couple of rare luxury presents: a gold Michael Kors handbag and a bottle of Chanel No 5 perfume, all of which was completely out of character for me as a charity shop regular.

But it's still not an easy life that I lead. Apart from my health problems, it's a dog-eat-dog business that I am working in and so many people have tried to drag me into the gutter along the way. There was a big hooha in February 2016 when somebody who was working for me at the time, doing my admin, grew lazy and sent out duplicate 'Letters from Heaven' to multiple people. When it came to light (after one recipient went to the tabloid newspapers), that person was sacked on the spot and the people involved were all refunded. Thankfully, my regular clients didn't doubt me and it didn't do any lasting damage.

Some of the same papers that carried the story accusing me of being a 'fake' were quick to publish stories of my numerous psychic successes, including footage of ghostly goings-on when I visited a notorious haunted house in nearby Pontefract in February 2017.

If I've learnt anything at all from my life experiences – both good and bad – it is that there comes a point in your life when you just have to let go and move on, even if you can't always quite forgive and forget. At 54 – about half a century since I first became a victim of my father's sexual abuse – I realise that there's no point in holding on to bitterness.

Joseph Joyce, who was released from prison on licence in October 2017 after serving only half of his sentence, is completely irrelevant to me now after my court victory. That doesn't mean that I am not angry and disgusted with the authorities, who ignored the letter I wrote urging them to keep him behind bars and, instead, allowed him to go free. I know that restrictions will be in place and that he'll always be on the Sex Offenders Register and closely watched; however, I also know first-hand what's he's capable of, and I am anxious about the possibility that he will somehow manage to harm other children.

My feelings towards my mother, who served half of her four-year sentence before being released, are more complicated. When she died of an arterial air embolism (an air bubble in an artery) in May 2017, I was confused and mixed up. I heard the news in the middle of the supermarket, in a phone call from my son Martin.

It's fortunate that Jack was with me, because I suffered a severe panic attack: my face drained of colour, my throat closed up and my tongue began to swell. I was in complete shock. My father and mother may have paid the price for what they did in the eyes of the justice system, but I am still left to live as best I can in the aftermath. Panic attacks are a lasting reminder of what they did to me; claustrophobia and agoraphobia are two others. Rheumatoid arthritis and high blood pressure are another two potential side effects. Yes, I received criminal injuries compensation after the court case (the princely sum of £22,000), but that meant nothing to me. All it did was enable me to help my children a bit financially and put a smile on their faces.

But back to my mum: all I can say is that she was my mum and I was her daughter and I loved her, but I hated her for what she allowed to happen. To be fair, she did send multiple sympathy cards and massive bouquets of flowers when Little Jack – who she'd never had as much time for as his siblings when he was alive – passed. My father sent nothing. *Despite everything, I always loved you*, my mother wrote to me. But I'd put up a solid wall to protect myself by then, and I refused point-blank to see her. What could she tell me that I hadn't heard in Leeds Crown Court? When she couldn't help me in my hour of grief, or see Little Jack in the chapel of rest as she so desperately wanted, I think it finished her. I honestly do.

I cannot commend her enough, though, for everything she did for my older children; sadly, her good relationship with some of them has affected their relationship with me. The court case split the whole family down the middle. I see my son Martin, but I rarely see or speak to Charmaine at all. I never see her three children and I've never seen her youngest child, one of my five grandchildren. It may be hard to understand, but I have to cling to the belief that my mum loved me, and I like to think that caring for my children was maybe her way of making amends for what happened to me. But who really knows why she allowed it to happen? Who can say? Maybe she was afraid of my father, or bullied into it by him. That's a question I will never have answered now. I do know that I made the right decision in not going to her funeral – a full requiem mass – and I have no regrets about that.

Nor do I have any regrets about not replying to her when her spirit came through to me several months after her passing. I was wide awake at the time, and I suddenly sensed her presence all around me. Although I couldn't see her, I could recognise her voice saying, "Paula love, it's me, your mam." It was weird: it was one of those days when I was struggling badly with my grief over Jack, and she picked up on it straight away.

"You won't make it past next Christmas if you don't pull yourself together, love," she warned. "Jack's doing fine over here. He's OK. You've got to live for your other children and your husband. You can't go on as you are."

Although I didn't acknowledge it, I knew she was right. Some days I'm so distraught over my loss and my past that I can't get up off the floor. While my Star People are always there to chivvy me along, saying, "You can do this, Paula," sometimes even that's not enough.

Make no mistake: the effects of the kind of abuse I suffered last a lifetime. If anything positive can be said about my lost, traumatic childhood, it is that it has made me more compassionate with people. I get satisfaction from helping others, and in a way that helps me to cope. I'm over the moon that, in Jack's name, we have donated thousands of pounds to the children's asthma charity Breathe for Cameron. And I can be lying on the floor, consumed with grief, but within an hour or two of picking myself up, glamming myself up and becoming Lillyanne Psychic Medium, I suddenly feel so much better providing comfort to bereft people online or during a telephone reading.

Even when writing this book, there was a dual aim. As well as wanting to show the world who Lillyanne Psychic Medium really is, I wanted to prove to other childhood abuse victims that they can become survivors like me, not victims. I didn't waive my anonymity about my ordeal after my court case and speak to the newspapers for my own benefit: I wanted to show that even if it happened many years ago, you can still report abuse and be taken seriously. Believe me, there's no better feeling than being believed and listened to after years of torment. Not even winning the jackpot on the Lottery could compare to it. The effects of the trauma won't just magically disappear afterwards, but you will be able to move forward and discover peace. One of my ways of coping even now is to head for the solace of the local graveyard whenever I want to quietly gather my thoughts and reflect on the traumatic life I've led. Sometimes I sit there peacefully among the graves for 15 minutes; sometimes it's an hour. Usually I come away feeling relaxed and rejuvenated. My husband and my soulmate, Jack, is always at my side these days, a permanent fixture. A graveyard is somewhere we can just sit, often in silence, holding hands and shaking our heads together over the past. To think that they said our relationship wouldn't last! Well, we've been tested to the limit and we've still proved all our critics wrong. Nobody can deny us that.

All in all, my story is a very sad one but it's one that I desperately wanted to tell when the time was right. And for me, the time is right now. Yes, it's been a tough journey all the way and I'm still travelling. But hey, look at me! I am still here and I'm still standing! And I'm now on a mission to empower others to do the same. Whether that's as Paula Bairstow, abused daughter, or Lillyanne Psychic Medium, it doesn't really matter.

My column in Soul & Spirit Magazine

Me, 2017

My granddaughter Lily and me

My grandson Devantae and son Ashley

My sons Martin and Ashley, granddaughter Lily and me

My son Martin and grandson Devantae

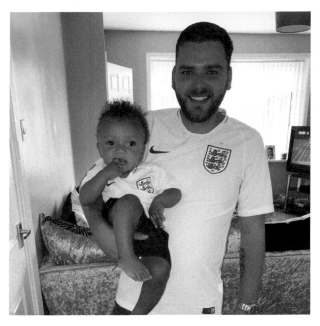

My son Ashley and grandson Devantae

My husband Jack and grandson Devantae

Ashley's partner Kyle and my grandson Devantae

15

A FEW WORDS FROM THE HEART

Paula's immediate family did not want this book to be published without a tribute from them to express their love and admiration for her. Here's what they had to say.

Husband Jack

When I met Paula, I connected with her straight away. I'd met younger girls and gone out with them in the past, but this was completely different.

I was always a shy guy, quite on edge with people, but once Paula walked in something just clicked. I thought she was stunning and I couldn't believe she'd had all those kids. I kept thinking, *She's perfect. Just perfect.* But it was more than that. It didn't feel like I was meeting her for the first time: it was like we'd been there before. As if we'd been together in a past life. Now I know we probably have. And I still feel the same way about her as I did all those years ago. I don't just love her now: I'm so proud of everything she's come through, as well, everything she's achieved. Paula, you're awesome.

Daughter Katy

My mum has had an exceptional life, and I honestly believe that she has endured pain that no human being should ever have to endure. Times have not been easy for her. She's had a string of bad luck, but she's always tried to manage it. And because of her strength, we've had some great times.

She's gone through so much pain and heartache that for her to be able to stand up and look at the world with such positive eyes is nothing short of an inspiration – to her family, to everyone.

My first thoughts as a kid of three years old – aside from the love I felt for my mum – were of how I hoped to be strong like her when I was older. If my mum could go through all that pain, I could stand up and be there for her.

Mum is undoubtedly a very strong lady, but she's also a handful! An absolute whirlwind! She sits in her favourite armchair, all sweet and innocent, but she's a ball of fire really. It's that fire inside her belly that's kept her going. That's why she's a survivor.

Sometimes that fire is a bit hot to handle, and you have to be a little bit tentative in the way you do so. That's not a criticism. You can't have it both ways: that fire is what's got her where she is today.

She isn't just a mother – she's much more than that. She's a counsellor, she's a wife, she's a best friend. It's not been easy between the two of us: we didn't have a relationship for a long time because I spent a lot of my late childhood and early adulthood living with my grandmother, Pauline. I remember wanting to live with her at 11 years old. Looking back, I think I was having some kind of breakdown at the time, and Nanna took me in. I didn't go to live in Hull with Mum and Jack, and we didn't have a relationship for a long time. From my point of view, we only bonded again when I got back from Bali at 31 years old, after becoming very ill (ironic, considering that I was going there for a health detox). I contracted dengue fever stage three and typhoid at the same time, and nearly died. Ashley and Kyle had to come to get me off this tiny Indonesian island that had no doctors and no hospital. I was very lucky to survive, but I'd go through it all 10 times over because if it hadn't happened, I wouldn't have been at home when the worst happened and Little Jack passed. I've always detached myself a bit because I had a hard time when I was younger. At 19 I went to France to be a campsite customer service rep, and then I did the same thing in Italy. Then, soon after returning home, I moved to Cyprus for six months. I don't think I've ever lost that feeling of wanting to go out and see the world and be free.

When I fell ill in July 2016, I had no plans to come home. I had flights booked to Cambodia. I was going to do Thailand and then New Zealand that year. I didn't plan on returning to this side of the world for a long time. It was a big shock to me, then, to lose my independent life and find myself at 31, waking up one morning back in my mum's spare single bed wearing one of her dodgy nightgowns! Disorientated, I came round to find her stroking my head. She was talking to me but neither of us can remember what she was saying. I think it's just called healing.

So for the first time since I was 11, I lived permanently with my mum for five months until I was well enough to go away again. Being with her shocked me: I realised that was only just beginning to find out about her quirky little ways. How she likes her eggs and her cup of tea and her ham sandwiches cut! We soon had our own little routine, where she'd sit on the bottom of the bed, light a cig, and chat to me. That made me think about my mum's life a lot.

I also knew that something had brought me home at that point. I haven't lived at home since I was 11, and at 31 here I was. I was thinking, *Why am I here?* I'd never feel out of place here because this is my home, where all my loved ones are, but I felt like a fish out of water. It didn't feel right. I felt really dishevelled. Looking back now, I am glad I was ill because it brought me home and gave me precious time with Little Jack. If I hadn't been sick, I wouldn't have come back to England and had that time to bond with Jack. It's precious time that I will never get again.

I could go on and on about my mum all day long! She's not just a mum and she never has been, ever since I can remember. She's always been a friend as well. Someone who's taught me life skills, which – particularly as a young woman growing up in the world – have been invaluable. My mum has been a massive influence on my life in terms of my choice of career – more so as I've got older. I worked in the property industry for nine years, but as I've got older, maturity has prompted me to start asking questions. You want to piece the puzzles together. It's one of the reasons I am studying psychology. I'd like to channel my experience and energy into helping people and putting something back into society. It just turns something really negative from my past into a positive experience. Has my mum been a great role model? Absolutely, but it's not all about me. It's so nice to see her doing so well in her own career. For years when we were growing up, we'd hear things like, "Your mum's a bit cuckoo. Your mum's this; your mum's that." There were always all these negative things said about our mum, all our lives. Nobody ever took what she does seriously until a couple of years ago. It's nice to see her finally getting what she deserves, and she's done it all herself. It's really humbling to see that, after putting up with all the negativity for so many years, things are finally working out for her. She deserves it. Now is her time.

Son Ashley

I honestly don't know what to say that will do Mum the justice she deserves. Yes, she inspires me, of course she does. The way that she's turned the bad things that have happened in her life into something so positive is a huge inspiration to me. I don't know how she's managed all she has, given her past, but I do like to think I've taken a lot of her strengths on board. I've definitely taken some of her attributes into my own life, into the way I live my life. I'm very spiritual myself because of Mum, and I'm a very sensitive and emotional person.

My dad Martin Flay and I have never really got on, even though I had a lovely relationship with his mum, my Nanna Dot. There's a wedge between us and I can't seem to break it down, but I wouldn't wish him any harm. I love my dad but in a different way to how I love my mum. Throughout my childhood, she always did her best to protect us and take care of us. We didn't have much, but she made sure we didn't go hungry and she always put us first.

Mum is a very, very strong woman but she's also a very funny, very warm and very interesting woman. She's very firm and always there to call you out if you're in the wrong and keep you on your toes. As I know! I wouldn't have you any other way, Mum.

Daughter Demi

My mum is a pinnacle of strength. Not many people could have dealt with so many awful situations in such a graceful way. She's stoic, strong, admirable and tough. She's also a great mum! Although she's always supportive, she's also very honest. She doesn't pull any punches. I think that's why the great British public – and the rest of her clients around the world – love her so much. I could go on and on about all the comforting little family traditions she keeps up: all the presents at Christmas and the house full of candles at Halloween. Not to mention the comfort food she makes us. Rice pudding with cinnamon!

It was always a strange thing at school having to explain to people the job that Mum did. Some would say, "My mum's a nurse," or, "My mum works in a shop," but I had to say, "My mum connects with the dead!" Some people were surprised, most were intrigued, but you'd get the odd idiot quick to call her names. As I've got older, I've appreciated more and more the comfort that she brings to people and I hope that one day I might be able to follow in her footsteps. It comes so naturally to her. It's not just her clients she cares about, though. It's all lost causes, from half-blind rescue kittens (she has nine cats) to the hedgehog and the birds in the garden that she always feeds. Quite simply, Mum is a brilliant role model. She's unique.

Ashley's partner Kyle

Paula is an amazing and exceptional woman. I don't know how she stays so brave. We bonded immediately when we first met, which was a surreal experience in itself.

The first time Ashley brought me home to introduce us, the family was sitting down watching her on a TV show about psychics. Bizarrely, I ended up sitting next to Paula whilst at the same time watching her on the TV screen! It was certainly something new. I'd never experienced anything like that before!

Laughing at my bemusement, Ashley told me, "Welcome to my dysfunctional family, Kyle!"

From that moment on, Paula and I just seemed to bounce off each other. My brother and I have always had an interest in the supernatural ourselves, so it was fascinating to meet Paula. Her greatest quality from my perspective, though, is probably her sense of humour, which is the same as mine: quite dry. The only slight downside is that up until meeting Paula, I'd always thought that I was the witty one!

Me and Buddy

My son Ashley and me

Me and my daughter Katy

My son Martin, me and granddaughter Lily

Me and my daughter Katy

Me and my daughter Katy

Me, my son Ashley and daughter Katy

My daughter Katy

16

A SPECIAL THANK YOU

There are so many people to thank for my own success and survival, but I'd like to concentrate on showing my gratitude to the people who did their utmost to save Little Jack on that terrible day.

A huge, heartfelt vote of thanks must go to the ambulance crew who were first on the scene, and the 15 staff at York Hospital who fought for two hours to try to save him. Their efforts were nothing short of valiant and, despite the sad outcome, enormously appreciated. More than words can say.

I also have to thank the community of Selby, including the kind staff of Sainsbury's and Wilko, who left so many lovely candles, flowers and tributes at the bench where Jack collapsed. His passing seemed to touch so many people.

Last but not least I have to give special mention to Little Jack's old schoolfriends Ben Varley and Will Coventry – his 'unbiological brothers', as Jack used to call them. They were all so close and it's lovely that they are still regular visitors to our home. It's true to say that they are more like family now than friends – even to the point of bringing me flowers on Mother's Day and Jack a card on Father's Day. No longer gawky schoolkids, they are young men now with futures. While it's been hard to see them growing up, starting careers and passing driving tests, knowing that Jack will never do any of those things, it is a great comfort all the same to retain that link. Little Jack would be so proud of them. Thank you, boys, from the very bottom of my heart.

17

OVER TO ALL YOU
LOVELY FANS

In my line of work there are always sceptics, so it's nice when you are able to show people what you can really do – as I did when I visited a house now known as the most haunted in England.

An ordinary semi-detached house on a council estate in nearby Pontefract, it is home to a poltergeist who, in the time of King Henry VIII, was a Cluniac monk hanged for the rape of a young girl. The home was built on the site where the scaffold was erected to hang him all those hundreds of years ago, meaning that he would have spent his final moments dangling from the end of a rope in the exact spot where the house was built. Centuries later, his spirit is still there – and is obviously very troubled, or he would not be causing the problems that he is.

What goes on inside the house is something else. Ghosthunters have been there many times before, and every one of them has reported strange experiences.

One lot who intended staying the night there got so frightened that they did a runner and refused to go back. They spent the night in a nearby hotel instead. Strange happenings at the house began in the 1960s, when a family called the Pritchards moved in and almost immediately experienced completely inexplicable events. Green foam would spew out of taps, lights would flash off and on, plants leapt up out of their pots, cupboards shook violently, photographs were slashed and an endless list of objects would levitate by themselves before being hurled about the place – including a solid oak sideboard. The house has become so famous that it was the subject of the 2012 horror movie *When the Lights Went Out,* and it was also investigated for the Halloween special of *Most Haunted Live* in 2015. I went there with Ashley and his partner Kyle, and they wanted me to summon the monk in a séance – which I did, a bit too successfully! I have to say that the house was really oppressive, with an atmosphere I have never felt before. There were definitely several spirits lurking in that home, and there was so much activity that we did not know where to start. There was also a host of strange smells, really awful ones that got you straight away. Then there was a face that appeared on the stairs behind us. It looked like a hooded figure, and that was where the Black Monk was most frequently seen, so I suppose it must have been him. I am a medium and I am used to this sort of thing, but it would have been terrifying for an ordinary member of the public. When we held the séance, I believe that I antagonised the energies in the room. I called them down and goaded the monk. To be honest there were numerous energies looking at me and following me. I knew I had to bring them to the table to interact with them. A picture was taken of me during the séance, which looked really creepy because it didn't look anything like me. People saw the shadow fall over my face, and it is brilliant that it was captured on camera and that my psychic abilities were proved to the public by the subsequent national newspaper coverage.

I had left by the time Ashley and Kyle started 'mirror scrying', where you call up the spirits and ask them to appear in the glass. All of a sudden Kyle seemed to freeze, his eyes went black and his face aged in seconds so that he looked like an old man. Ashley was really worried, especially when he kept calling Kyle's name and got no response. Kyle was completely zoned out. I think the spirit had taken him over and, as I explained to the newspaper, that is a really dangerous situation because it can cause chaos. It was getting close to a possession. People entering there should always have a qualified medium with them because in a possession the spirit can take you over completely. If it possesses you then anything could happen. There is a real danger that the person possessed could go into cardiac arrest, or that the spirit could cause them to smash the place up. It is not nice at all, and it can be really scary, but thankfully things did not reach that stage. Kyle is convinced that he caught an image of the monk in the mirror, and that is quite normal for mediums like me because the spirits are really powerful. I would have been more disappointed if we had not captured anything. Some people say it is all hype and that this house cannot be haunted, but I can tell you there is certainly something there.

I get a real kick out of getting the kind of results I got in Pontefract, but the real joy I get from my work is in helping the living. I receive messages of support from around the world for my psychic readings. The letters and emails I am sent make everything I do feel worthwhile. Take this one from Jessica Young: *'I had a question for Lillyanne tonight and it was: do you see a house move soon? I haven't stopped smiling since because she said she absolutely does see a move, a bit further away from where I am now. I 100% know what she means because it could mean that I'm going back to my home town. I'm over the moon with the reading. I also had two cards pulled out and they were spot on. I recommend anyone to have a reading with Lillyanne because she is a very, very gifted lady. Thank you so, so much.'*

Dawn Haron told her Facebook friends, *'Highly recommend. She's done me a couple of readings in the past and been very accurate with stuff only I knew about. I'd not told her anything about me at all. Great lady as well x'*

Some people make the connection between what I have told them and what they experience themselves after my reading. Sian Griffiths wrote, *'So after my messages with Lillyanne this morning, I have seen something really funny and it's never happened before. After she told me my Grandad contacted me through her, he was giving me some lovely words to try and pull myself together after my mental health had been playing up so much. Well I managed to confirm who it was and that I was at his graveside two weeks ago. This evening, around half an hour ago, I had a visit from a lovely bird using its beak to knock on my window, so I watched it. It fell off my window ledge and then it came back again, knocking on the window. When I went outside to throw some bread for the birds, the little birdie went away because it got my attention like it wanted me to love it. It's the first time ever this has happened and I'm so surprised. I have left my window open now to see if the little birdie comes back.'*

Some people are just content with knowing that I have really forged a connection between them and a loved one. Tammy Macneall told me, *'OMG I love you. When you did my phone reading, you had me crying just hearing that my nan was with me. Thank you so much! People, she's ACE.'*

Nichole Ellis spoke to one of my team, and she was happy with what we were able to do for her. She said, *'Thank you to Maureen who I have been talking to on the IM. Everything I've spoke to her about has come back with something she could not have known about. It has taken a huge weight off my shoulders.'*

All of us are really happy when people respond positively to what we have told them. This is a team job and we all work hard, as this correspondence proves. Pauley Colhoun-Matthews told us, *'I have just had an amazing phone reading with Caroline B, pin 2533. She was not only spot on, she gave some great advice as well. Thank you Caroline B, and thank you Lillyanne Psychic Medium.'* Mary Murphy was equally pleased with the team: *'Just had a reading from the lovely Atma… she was fantastic. Picked up on a lot of things going on in my life now. Thank you.'*

Meanwhile I received this message from Linda Glover-Hutchinson: *'What a wonderful reading from you tonight Lillyanne. You were so spot on. I could see my son standing behind your left shoulder!! He is a very cheeky boy and he obviously loves you as much as I do. You are the real deal, lovely lady. Your Jack is so proud of you!!'*

Serena Elson said to me, *'Just got my July Outlook and once again you have smashed it! It already makes so much sense and what was sent in my texts is already starting to happen! Every single one of your text readings have made so much sense!'*

Tamra Louise Hammond wrote, *'Had a lovely wee telephone reading from Lillyanne and everything she said was perfect. Thank you so much. Love and light to you all.'*

Leanne Keown said, *'LILLY I'm just beginning my journey. I'm super excited to follow this path with spirit. You told me to listen and I am. Thanks Lilly for the advice.'*

Nichola Corrigan: *'Thank you Lillyanne for the reading tonight. It meant so much to my eight-year-old daughter and to me, as life has been hard and chaotic for a few years. But knowing we are on the right path to better things is amazing xx'*

Here's Ally Morgan: *'Forgot to mention, I'm from Jersey in the Channel Islands. I think you're totally amazing, and just listening to you helps me to feel calm. L&L X.'*

And here's Claire Mullen: *'I had a lovely text reading from*

Lilly a couple of days ago. It has given me the direction I needed Thank you again xx'

Georgia Stamp confessed, *'Every time I watch you I get goosebumps! Xx'* While a very naughty Kim Garey admitted, *'Hello lovely Lilly, I've bunked off work to be with you today X'* Deborah Maher told me, *'Thank you for your amazing reading and guidance. Everything that was said was 100% spot on. Thank you.'*

Kerry Ann Quarterley was going through a difficult patch when she got in touch, and I was so glad to help. *'Hey Lilly and team, about a week or so ago I asked for a guidance reading and Lilly told me to say no to a relationship – not as in a partner but a family member. I couldn't understand why, but now I know and I've had to say no because there is so much going on in my family life. My girls come first. She also said things are going to start moving fast and again she was right! My baby girl turned one on 30th June, she took her first ever steps and constantly wants to be on her feet but also my eldest daughter is disabled. We are going through forms for her for next September. 100% spot on, thank you Lilly you're so gifted. Thank you for all your time and effort xx'*

Some people who come to me are quite naturally sceptical, but I hope I am able to change their minds. Rhiannon Minter was someone who was not sure, so it was a delight when I picked this up in my mailbox: *'Lilly your text message tonight meant so much to me. It made me so emotional and scared at the same time. It's lovely to hear from a loved one and it made me look differently at people who do readings. I believe … wow, wow, wow! Thank you.'*

We do, of course, often have to deal with tragedies, but even in the midst of grief we try and bring comfort and hope wherever we can. Liana Burgin got in touch to say, '*My step father committed suicide. What you just said bought tears, but happy ones… It's so comforting to know that they get so much support on the other side. Love you my guardian angel…*'

But it's not all about readings and keeping in touch with the dead. The living should mean as much to us as the spirits that have gone before, and it's the people around us who should be our first priority. That is why I, and the rest of my family, try and do the best we can for others. It was a delight to receive this message from Kez Walters, who appealed to us for help in raising money to buy an air purifier for her son. She wrote: '*Me and Connor want to say a massive thank you to Lillyanne and her son who are both amazing people. I can't explain how grateful and touched I am at your kind generosity in providing Connor with this air purifier. For nearly three years, Birmingham Children's Hospital have tried to get funding to provide Connor with an Airsonnet (air purifier) but could not get it. The Airsonnet company let Connor have one on loan for six months. It improved his allergies a lot and helped with his asthma. He was the first child to trial it. As soon as it went, he started having allergic reactions again, waking up with swollen eyes, sneezing all night. His respiratory team suggested I try a Go Fund Me page to raise money to get the Dyson air purifier. I didn't really want to do one as I didn't want people to think I was begging for money. After a few weeks I decided to do it and I messaged Lillyanne to see if she could share the link on her page. Within minutes Lillyanne and her son were on the phone to me and wanted to buy the air purifier for Connor. I was shocked and emotional. Nobody has ever done anything this nice for us. It will be a massive help for Connor. He's got brittle asthma, multiple allergies and eczema. I can't thank you enough. You are very special to me and my boy now.'*

Enough said.

My daughter Joanne and son Ashley

Me and my daughter Katy

My daughter Demi with Alfie

My daughter Joanne and son Ashley

My daughter Demi and son Ashley

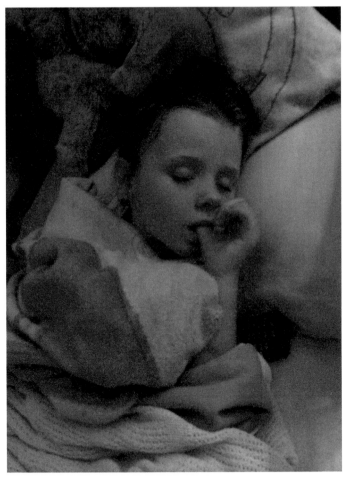

My granddaughter Lily

Take kids to park 🤍✨🤍

My grandchildren Devantae and Lily

My granddaughter Lily

My daughter Katy

My grandson Nathan

My son Little Jack and grandson Nathan

My grandson Devantae

Me, my husband Jack, Ashley and Kyle with the fantastic team at Allstar Psychics